The Burwell
Fossil Diggings

Bernard O'Connor

Bernard O'Connor

It was two Burwell men, the doctor, Mr Lucas, and the miller, John Ball, who were the first in the area to recognise the economic potential of a very different use of the fenland. Traditionally the main occupations were fishing, hunting, cutting reeds and digging clunch and turf. A new occupation was to follow an anonymous farmer taking some fossils he'd found on his property to show Rev. John Henslow, the professor of Botany at St. John's College, Cambridge. One of his students, Charles Darwin, was to throw the academic world into a spin with his controversial theories of natural selection and evolution as well as increase the Victorians' interest in anthropology, palaeontology and geology. But it was another of Rev. Henslow's students, Charles Kingsley, who recorded the importance of the fossils.

"He saw, being somewhat of, a geologist and chemist, that they were not, as fossils usually are, carbonate of lime, but phosphate of lime - bone earth. He said at once, as by inspiration, "You have found a treasure - not a gold-mine, indeed, but a food-mine. This bone earth, which we are at our wit's end to get for our grain and pulses; which we are importing, as expensive bones, all the way from Buenos Ayres. Only find enough of them, and you will increase immensely the food supply of England and perhaps make her independent of foreign phosphates in case of war".

(Anonymous note in Ipswich Museum, Coprolite File)

A treasure? A food-mine? Such a response must have astounded the farmer. It is undocumented whether the farmer was from Burwell but, as we shall see, quite possible. Professor Hailstone of Bottisham reported that fossils were found beneath the fenland peat as early as 1816. (Hailstone, Rev. J. (1816), 'Outlines of the Geology of Cambridgeshire', Phil. Trans. Royal.

Soc., pp.243-250) Their discovery was related to a less common but important fenland occupation, locally called "claying". This involved the digging of small pits through the "moor" or "bear's muck", as the bog-earth was called, to reach the clay. This lay between two and ten feet (0.74m. - 3.7m.) below the surface. Wearing waterproofed boots the diggers would use a sharp, cutting-edged shovel to dig through the peat, a light wooden scoop to get rid of drainage water and an axe or "bill" to excavate the clay beneath. The top metre of clay was thrown to the sides of the pit and then mixed into the peat.

The material turned up by this "claying" occasionally included fossils of what were thought to be bears and oxen. When Burwell Fen started to be drained in the early-1800s the excavation of drainage ditches or "lodes" exposed an extensive bed of fossils. The farmer, John Ball, noticed that the turnips he grew on the clayey, fossil deposit that had been mixed into his peat soil produced dramatically better yields than the crops on fields he hadn't clayed. The local doctor, Mr. Lucas, explained that the "extraordinary liveliness" was related to the high phosphate content of the fossils. ('The Farming of Cambridgeshire,' Royal Agric.Soc.1847, p.71; Lucas, C. (1930), 'The Fenman's World - Memories of a Fenland Physician,' (Norwich), p.25)

Whether the doctor was aware that in 1842 Rev. Henslow had found a similar fossil bone bed in the Suffolk Crag in Felixstow is not known. On exploring a newly exposed cliff face following a landslip, Henslow had found some long, thin, smooth brown fossils that he thought were "coprolites" - fossilised droppings. Another religious academic, Rev. William Buckland coined the term "coprolites", in 1829. He was the Dean of Westminster and Oxford University's first professor of Geology and Mineralogy and had found the fossils of ichthyosaurus exposed by a landslip in the cliffs at Lyme Regis in Dorset. Among them he identified its fossil excreta, which he termed them "coprolites" from the Greek "kopros" meaning dung and "lithos" meaning stone. In a lecture to the

Society for the Advancement of British Science in Cambridge in 1845 Henslow talked about the Suffolk coprolites. He suspected that if the fossil bones were used as manure then they could be a matter of "commercial proposition".

At this time Great Britain was reported to be *"like a ghoul, scouring the continent for bones to feed its agriculture"*. Such was the demand that sun-dried bones from the Egyptian deserts, mummified cats from Egyptian pyramids, the contents of Sicilian catacombs and even bones from the battlefields of the Crimea were added to the manure manufacturers' "dens". To have such an extensive fossil bone bed available locally explained one manufacturer offering £14 a ton for the Felixstow fossils! This was made in ignorance of their real value. In 1842 John Bennet Lawes, a Hertfordshire landowner, had patented the technique of using phosphatic materials to produce chemical manure. Much to the annoyance of his mother and friends he went into business and set up a manure factory. He must have disappointed his fiancée as he cancelled a Grand Tour for a honeymoon in favour of a trip on the Thames where he spotted an ideal site for his factory at Barking. One the phosphatic material was ground to a powder he mixed it with vitriol, the Victorian term for sulphuric acid, to produce super phosphate of lime - the first chemical manure. Dried and bagged Lawes' "super" was advertised in the agricultural and gardening press at up to £7.00 a ton to the growing number of farmers keen to increase yields. This was about half the price of the other successful manure on the market - guano - phosphate-rich bird droppings, which in 1838 had been imported into Liverpool from the Pacific Islands off Chile. It proved particularly effective on root crops on clay soils, dramatically increasing turnip yields. As a fodder crop, this helped to provide winter-feed and allowed farmers better prices for their cattle. Capitalising on his patent Lawes charged other manure manufacturers five shillings (£0.25) a ton to use his method of making superphosphate.

When chemical analysis of the Suffolk fossils showed them to have a phosphate content of between 50% - 60%, manure manufacturers recognised a cheap, raw material and an alternative to bones. Coprolite contractors approached the owners of coprolite land with an offer of a royalty for every ton that they were able to raise from the fields. This varied between four and fifteen shillings. (£0.20 - £0.75) a ton, depending on the phosphate content, depth, extent, dip, cleanliness, accessibility to a water source for washing and transport as well as a nearby wharf or railway siding and of course competition from other contractors. When the manure manufacturers were paying about £2.00 a ton for the coprolites in the 1840s and 50s considerable profits were being made. A gang of men and boys, sometimes, the farmers' agricultural labourers, were taken on at piece rate to do the work and the contractor arranged the sale and transport of the washed fossils to the manure manufacturers. In some cases, freeholders and tenant farmers alike got their own labourers to dig them out of the crag and sold them to coprolite merchants or direct to manure manufacturers.

It was often a job undertaken in the winter months, once the harvest was in. The fossils were dug out and thrown into the back of tumbrils, wide-bodied wooden carts and hauled down to the sea or river's edge where they were dumped ready for washing. A straw windbreak was erected for the men to shelter from the freezing easterly winds off the North Sea. The technology involved was simple. A cut was made into the bank and a rectangular wooden frame was installed. The fossils were emptied into wooden crates, which were immersed in this frame and pushed from end to end with a pole. Once clean they were emptied into barrows, wheeled up planks and emptied into barges or shallow-draught lighters. These carried up to twenty-five tons, up the River Orwell to manure works in Ipswich or up the Thames to London. So started a new extractive industry - a branch of agricultural mining.

Ground into a powder and dissolved in sulphuric acid was what happened to the vast bulk of the deposit. However, the better specimens were sold to the geologists and fossil collectors who haunted the pits. Ipswich Museum has a fascinating collection. In this area the locals thought that they were "bear's muck", "lizard's muck", "mammoth dung" and even "dinosaur droppings". A retired major from Reach argued that they are similar to sun-dried wildebeest droppings he'd found when the floodwaters had receded from the banks of the Zambezi! Whilst some of the fossils certainly resemble fossilised rectal contents the Victorian geologists, who were fascinated by the variety being unearthed, rejected the idea. They argued that they were phosphatic nodules from the Cretaceous period, about 120 - 65 million years ago. The bed contained not just the sun-dried, phosphatised droppings of creatures living in the seas and on the coastal plains of Cretaceous Britain but also the teeth, bones, scales and claws of dinosaurs. Iguanodon, megalosaur, dakosaur, dinotosaur, scelidosaur and craterosaur were found, as well as the marine reptiles of ichthyosaurus, pliosaurus and plesiosaurus and the bird pterodactyl. But it wasn't just dinosaurs. There were fossils of prehistoric whale, shark, crocodiles, turtles, sponges, shellfish and a wide variety of marine organisms - the most common being ammonites. There were the remains of land animals too. Elephant, hippopotamus, rhinoceros, oxen, hyena, bear and horse were excavated as well as fossilised trees. It is thought, however, that these mammal fossils were "discovered" when the diggers cut through much more recent sediments to reach the far more ancient Greensand sediments further down.

But what had produced this enormous graveyard from about 94 Million years ago? It is thought that volcanic carbon dioxide and other poisonous gases released from flood basalts occasioned by tectonic activity along the Mid-Atlantic Ridge and elsewhere affected the animal's respiratory system. It produced a high-stress environment and many died quite quickly. It is also thought that a sudden rise in sea level, maybe a gigantic tidal wave, destroyed the coastal habitats along the northern edge of the 'London-Brabant Platform' and wiped out much of the food chain. The wave erosion also uncovered earlier fossils buried under older sediments and these reworked remains accumulated on the seabed amongst the remains of the recent dead organisms. Here they became phosphatised in the warm shallow coastal embayments and subsequent burial under the sand and later the chalk led to the creation of an extensive fossil bed. The majority of the deposit was small, black amorphous lumps, indiscernible as fossils. Part of it contained a large volume of inorganic phosphatic concretions; some built up around a fossil cast.

Not only were the contents of the bed of intense interest to the students of the new sciences of geology and palaeontology but also the religious Victorian academics hotly debating Darwin's controversial theories. Many Victorian drawing rooms had their glass display cabinet with its fossil collection and the country's major museums had shelves filled with fossils from the Suffolk Crag and Cambridgeshire Greensand. But the main reason why they were extracted was not for the pursuit of academic knowledge but commercial reasons.

Dr. Lucas may well have heard about Rev. Henslow's Cambridge speech or read about it in the local press. Aware of the potential demand by manure manufacturers and maybe even knowing the farmer he undoubtedly suspected that the Burwell deposit could also be a matter of "commercial proposition". Their shallow depth beneath the fenland peat just above the gault clay would allow them to be raised without very high labour costs. The proximity of Burwell Lode allowed easy access by barge or lighter to Popes Corner - the confluence of the Ouse and the Cam - and then via Ely, Littleport and Downham Market onto King's Lynn and then transhipped to Ipswich or London.

With an eye for speculation and without having first seen it, he bought some eleven acres of Burwell Fen. The locals thought he had taken leave of his senses. A month later, so the story goes, he went by boat up Burwell Lode with "an interested party" to locate the deposit. After rowing for some time, they reached a point about a mile west of the village where the potential buyer was handed a "sprit" and told to push it into the land below the boat. (Gathercole, A.F. (1959), 'Fenland Village,' Fisons Journal, No.64 Sept. pp.24-9; Suffolk County Record Office (SCRO) HC 438.8728/269)

The depth of the seam was not noted but the locals were astounded when he sold the plot and the coprolites beneath it for £1,000. Realising almost £100 per acre was a phenomenal profit, given that agricultural rents ranged from about £0.50 - £2.00 an acre. The "interested party" was William Colchester, one of the Suffolk manure manufacturers who also had investments in brick manufacturing and ships. That year, 1846, he expanded his Suffolk manure business with a new manure works in Ipswich. According to a later geological paper he had raised 500 tons by 1847. (Lucas, C. (1930), op.cit; Reid, C. (1890), 'Nodule Bed,' Memoirs of the Geological Survey (Mem.Geol.Surv.) p.16)

A new technological development was introduced in Burwell that allowed the coprolites to be washed more efficiently. Once they had been brought to the surface, Charles Lucas, the doctor's son, described the next procedure: -

> "The first thing to do was to throw up a hill in the middle of the ground, and this was done by first erecting a post about ten or twelve feet long, and throwing the (top) soil around it to a height of eleven or twelve feet and of thirty feet in diameter. Three feet from the centre a ring would be formed six to eight feet wide and four feet deep. This would be paved with bricks and the sides would be sheets of iron. On one side of the hill a platform was made from a wooden tank, to which was connected a pump eighteen feet long; a pipe from the tank would go with the ring and opposite the tank was a trapped outlet, and on the outer side of the hill a square of about two chains would be earthed up a little to form a sort of pan. From the central post a wooden arm would be attached about twelve to fourteen feet long; to this would be attached a wimpole tree, to which a horse would be yoked. Connected to the centre of the post would be a light rail which was fixed to the horse bridle to keep the horse always in its track; from the arm would be

suspended two iron harrows which ran well in on the bottom of the ring. When the soil containing the fossils was wheeled up to the ring a sufficient quantity of water would be let in. As the horse went round a creamy fluid would be produced and the fossils would drop on the floor. Then the trapped outlet would be opened and the creamlike fluid, called "slurry" would flow into pans. This operation having been repeated a number of times the fossils on the floor would be washed clear of earth and weighed up".

(Lucas, C. op.cit. p31)

The cost of constructing these mills when they were first developed cost £100 but by 1875 the *"coprolite contractors had become so expeditious that a hill could be put up for £5!"* (Ibid.) The sight of such mills was recorded in a tourist's account of a trip from Burwell to Newmarket

"As we return from Burwell our eyes rest on several raised circular enclosures, round which a number of often grey horses are almost ceaselessly walking. These are the mills erected for washing the fossils. These fossils or coprolites are valuable on account of the calcic phosphate contained in them".

(Eade, David, (18..), 'Rambles in Cambridgeshire,' (Soham) p.48)

Given the profits to be made, John Ball made arrangements to raise them from land belonging to his father, the local MP, Mr. E. Ball. He had his labourers raise them from the fen and converted them for agricultural use himself. According to the Victoria County History's account of the parish he

"...undertook all stages of the process himself. Having dug his coprolites, he flung them into his mill, placed the resulting powder in a mashtub and added sulphuric acid. He found that a biscuit formed, which he then pounded

up and spread on his fields with excellent results".
(V.C.H. 'Cambs.,' vol.ii, Burwell)

This operation is reported to have taken place in his Big Mill Windmill in the village, the first mill reported to be put to such use. (O.S. GR.59116660; Cambridgeshire Archaeology Department, dbase 06495) It would have entailed him changing the millstones to the hard buhrstone in order to grind the coprolites. There was a conflicting report, however, which suggested that Jim Faben, another Burwell man, did the first "mix". He is supposed to have mixed it in a farmhouse in the village, using a wooden paddle to stir the ingredients in a wooden half-tub. (Lucas, op.cit.)

Other members of the Ball family, Richard and Thomas, set themselves up in business in 1851 selling both the coprolite and their home-made superphosphate. Richard also farmed the Charity land and with the family interests in brickmaking and fertilisers they were true 19th century entrepreneurs. (Grove, R. (1976), 'The Cambridgeshire Coprolite Mining Rush,' Oleander Press, p7; Gathercole, A.F., op.cit.p.29)

The first actual record of the diggings was in the autumn of 1850 when the Cambridge Chronicle reported an auction of three and a half acres of coprolite land. Whether Mr. Colchester, Mr. Ball or another prospective entrepreneur purchased the lot was not recorded. (Cambridge Chronicle, 29th October, 1850 p.1)

The 1851 census showed the population had doubled in size since the turn of the century and that there had been an increase of 347 since 1841, the largest increase that century. This must have been attributed to the diggings. There was no reference to coprolite or fossil digging as an occupation that year. This can be explained by the fact that, in the early years of the industry, on small-scale operations, it tended to be agricultural labourers who did the work, once the harvest was in. By spring they'd get on with the farm work and so didn't term themselves fossil or coprolite diggers. Generally, once the fields had been drained and the harvest was in, on wintry mornings bands of man and boys would have been seen wandering onto the fen to spend the day digging up these fossils. One observer, a Mr. Spence, having witnessed the scene, gave a talk to a group in Manchester and revealed how much more profitable an occupation it was compared to farming.

> "The locality from which the specimens of the vein and fossils were obtained was the village of Burwell, twelve miles from Cambridge, and on the estate of E. Ball, Esq. MP, for Cambridgeshire. Here the fen is studded over with the diggings and washing apparatus, the population all actively engaged, and wages usually at or under twelve shillings a week are advanced to fifteen shillings, and parties working by the piece are earning twenty shillings a week. Thousands of tons will be extracted before the ensuing Spring, the season of chief demand for the fossil for artificial manure".

(Spence, (1857) 'On Coprolites,' Proceedings of the Literary and Philosophical Society, Manchester, p.3)

He estimated that the vein stretched along the entire length of the fen in a band not less than a quarter of a mile wide, with a yield of between 150 and 200 tons per acre. One sample, he said, had over 70% phosphate of lime, a fact that further explained Messrs. Colchester and Ball's interest. Prior to the diggings, an acre of land would not have sold at more than twenty pounds and, having been dug and restored to farming, its value doubled. The thorough digging over of the field added essential nutrients to the top and subsoil. With contractors willing to pay such high royalties it naturally attracted the intense interest of farmers and landowners alike.

At the end of October 1857, ten years after the start of the industry, the Cambridge Independent Press included a report on

"BURWELL COPROLITES - these fossils have been discovered to a considerable extent on the Burwell Fen lands, which have created quite a sensation in the village. Many persons have commenced digging, and it is not improbable that a mill will be erected in the village for grinding them. Labourers are paid 2s.6d. per day for digging them and they are not overpaid, considering the labour required. At a sale of land in Burwell this week, it realised £70 per acre although the same land a few years ago would have fetched only a nominal sum".

(Cambridge Independent Press (CIP), 24th Oct.1857)

A couple of months later another plot on Burwell Fen came onto the market. The same newspaper advertised it in such a way as to appeal to those with money to invest in the plant and machinery need for such an operation.

"BURWELL, CAMBS. IMPORTANT TO CAPITALISTS 10 Acres of land abounding in valuable BEDS OF COPROLITES. Mr Feist has been favoured with instructions from the Feoffees of Burwell Charity Lands to Let by Auction at the Fox Inn, Burwell on Thursday 28th January 1858 for a term of two years to commence on the 29th inst. (subject to such conditions as will be produced at the time of letting.) the right of entry into and upon 10 acres of land lying in Burwell Fen abutting N on the Lord's Droveway; E on High Town Droveway; W on Land of the Crown; and S on land of the said Feoffees. For the purpose of raising Coprolites therefrom; a Lessee paying to the said

Feoffees a certain sum for every ton raised and carried off the Land".

(CIP, 16th Jan.1858)

Subsequent evidence suggests that Mr. Ball won the agreement. Once the fossils had been located, the landowner or farmer would have either used their existing labourers to raise them if they were only found on only a small scale, or, for larger operations like this, tenders were invited. Manure manufacturers, like Mr. Colchester, would have made a bid via an agent, signed an agreement, engaged a foreman and hired a gang of men and boys.

Another advantage this area had was the availability of a skilled group of labourers experienced in excavating the clay and the clunch. The latter had been used as a building material for centuries and was also burned to make lime in local kilns. Turf cutters also had digging experience so, when the coprolites were discovered, it was likely some of the more experienced clay, clunch and turf cutters readily found employment. No doubt some of the work gangs would have been organised by "fen tigers". It was common fenland practice for a gang master to get paid a set rate for a piece of work and then employ young children to do the work as it was cheaper than adult labour. However, they also took on gangs of men. The work involved in coprolite digging was too hard for youngsters. They tended to be more involved in the washing and sorting. In parishes like nearby Wicken and Potton in Bedfordshire, large numbers of women and girls were employed. Although none were recorded in the census returns it may well have been that in the intervening years large numbers were taken on or that they described it as agricultural labour.

There was concern about the exploitation and poor working conditions of the children. In 1866 Rev. J. B. James, the rector of Gamlingay, provided fascinating details of these conditions. He wrote to Hon. E. Portman, the commissioner in charge of the government's investigations into child labour.

"The coprolite diggings in our neighbourhood have occupied very many of our boys, many of whom earn at them 8s. and 9s. a week, which is more than the farmers can give them."
SANDY.

50. Mr. Coulson. - "Girls of 7 years up to 18 years are employed in the coprolite works. The work is taken by the piece; they get a sum per ton for picking over the fossils. A girl of ten years would earn 7s. a week by day work, but much more by piece work. The state of education among them is very low; some can read, hardly any can write. The parents also are very uneducated. This and the adjoining district of Polton [sic] is a gardening tract; children are much employed in large numbers in peeling onions and such like work. I have seen gross cases of immorality and indecency, even among the smaller children, at leisure moments at the coprolite mills when waiting for the carts, and have heard much bad language, which is readily learnt by the young from constantly hearing it round them. The foremen do not check them. The sexes should be separated at the mills, by means of different sheds, or even by separate mills for boys and girls. In one instance the foreman keeps a public house, where the wages are paid, and the men and children are allowed to have as much drink as they like during the week on credit, and the money is deducted on pay night. These children have no time for learning, except in the evening."
ARLESEY

46a. "There are three sets of coprolite works, three brickyards and a cement works, which have caused a great increase in population, especially in summer, when many houses are crowded. Coprolite employs a good many men, many of whom are *strangers. Coprolite works employ some boys, leading horses.*

BIGGLESWADE UNION.

"Coprolite works and brick fields may be added to the causes given by Mr. Weale for the overcrowding and use of bad cottages in the neighbourhood of Biggleswade."

(BCRO CRT 160/140 Parliamentary Papers 1867-8 XVII
'1st Report of the Commissioners on the Employment of Children, Young Persons and others in Agriculture', pp.
343, 506, 518)

Mr Postman's summary added further details about the work in Cambridgeshire and showed that Mr. Peel had attempted to provide the youngsters with the rudiments of education.

COPROLITE DIGGINGS.

"131. There is in Cambridgeshire much employment for the young of both sexes of the agricultural labouring classes at the coprolite works. These works are increasing in number, the price paid for the right of digging is from £80. to £100. An acre, it being agreed that the land shall be restored to the owner levelled and in a state fit for cultivation. The digging work is done by men and grown lads; boys are employed in wheeling barrows, and children of both sexes in sorting the fossils in the mills. Wages are high, boys can earn 8s. and 9s. A week, and a girl of 10 years of age earn 7s. a week by day work, but more by the piece, the payment for picking over the fossils being usually so much per ton... The state of education among these children is very low, and testimony is given as to the existence of gross immorality and indecency, no care being taken to separate the sexes at the mills.

On enquiring in the neighbourhood of Sandy and Potton, and elsewhere, I could not learn that any steps had been taken by the inspectors of factories to bring the provisions of the Workshop Act to bear on this industry, but it is possible that ere this the subject has occupied their attention.

MR PEEL'S SCHOOL.

132. Mr. Peel, MP, of Sandy, has built a shed conveniently situated for a certain number of these works, which is used for dinner, when hot coffee, &c. are provided at a low price, and for evening school. It is under the superintendence of Mr. Coulson, who reads to them at mealtimes, and gives religious and secular instruction. I attended an evening meeting of these children, when upwards of 80 of both sexes were present, who had been regular attendants at the school and regularly employed at the works, and as far as I could judge from the single opportunity, I feel sure that Mr. Peel and his coadjutor have every reason to be satisfied with the success of their missionary labours among this otherwise neglected population."

(Ibid. p.108)

In many of the clunch pits dug in and around Burwell the coprolite seam would have been exposed. Instead of being used to fill up the ruts in the roads, as they had been in the past, the coprolites were worked at the same time and put to more profitable use. However, not all the bed proved profitable. The prices paid for them fluctuated. One Burwell pit, Victoria Quarry, located between the windmills at Burwell High Town, the nodules were found 12 feet down (4.44m.) but they weren't profitable. This pit was worked in 1878 when a geological paper reported

"...none of these beds are used for building and the nodule bed is carted away as rubbish for it will not

burn into lime. The nodules are similar to those found at Reach and described by Prof. Hailstone. These nodules were called "brassel" by the workmen and is only quarried to be carted into the fens for road metal for it does not burn to a good lime".

(Pennings and Jukes Brown, (1881), 'Geology of the Neighbourhood of Cambridge,' Mem. Geol. Surv. p.46)

It is probable that the phosphate content of this particular bed was too low. The bed was not continuous and its thickness varied too. The sketch in the illustrations shows a digger at work in a pit where the bed undulates considerably. When the fossil was laid down on an uneven seabed it left the deepest and most phosphatic seams in the hollows.

By the mid-1850s the coprolite bed was found to extend along the fen edge as far north as Ely and southwest to the other side of Cambridge. Mr. Lucas' success in land speculation prompted him to buy coprolite land in other areas and then make a profit by selling the digging rights to interested contractors. In March 1858 another landowner, Mr. Allix, was approached by a Mr. Galley about the possibility of raising the coprolite from his estate. The services of Clement Francis, a Cambridge solicitor who had recently purchased the Quy Hall estate, were called for. He was much involved in coprolite agreements and advised Mr. Allix to allow his tenant farmer, Mr. Mason, to raise them from 18a.2r.3p. in the fen. It was felt that the land would be better restored for cultivation after the diggings had ceased by the farmer whose livelihood depended on the quality of restoration. What royalty was paid per ton is unknown. (Cambridgeshire County Record Office (CCRO. R59/27/1/2; CCRO. Francis & Co. Bill Books 1858 p.341; See author's accounts of Bassingbourn, Ashwell)

Village gossip about the profits to be made must have prompted other landowners with fen skirtland to have it tested. It was then advertised in the local press. In May 1858 the

Cambridge Independent Press included this advert.

> "**BURWELL. COPROLITE DIGGING IN FEN**. - *29 acres of valuable skirt and Fen land to be sold by auction by C. Mainprice, at the 'Fox Inn', Burwell, on Monday, the 17th of May 1858 at six o'clock in the evening (by direction of the trustees for sale under the will of the late Mr. William Durrant). The land is all Tithe-free, and from its close proximity to grounds abounding with coprolites, is exceedingly valuable*".
>
> (CIP 8th May, 1858, p.5)

The success of the industry had attracted considerable attention. On the same day the Cambridge Chronicle included the following article.

> "**BURWELL**. *Good wages digging coprolites which now carried on extensively in Fen. - The digging of coprolites is now carried on very extensively in this and the adjoining fens and has furnished abundant employment for a vast number of labourers during the spring and past winter. The men go from distant parishes and get good wages but are beginning to discover that regular and moderate pay at home is much better for themselves and their families*".
>
> (Cambridge Chronicle, (CC) 8th May 1858,p.5)

The message was clear. The local correspondent didn't want a mass exodus of able-bodied men leaving the area. As shall be seen there was considerable concern about the numbers of diggers moving into some parishes. In early May 1858, one of the diggers, guilty of raping a married woman, was sentenced to three years hard labour. This story must have spread amongst the diggers and was probably responsible for the men's better behaviour the following week at Reach Fair.

> "**600 Diggers In The Neighbourhood - Reach Fair**. *The public houses got well patronized; and what is more,*

good order seemed to prevail amongst the coprolite diggers numbering nearly 600 in the neighbourhood, and we hear of no disturbances taking place of any consequence. This may be considered due, partly, to the good and excellent precaution and management of Inspector Dade, of this division who had several officers on the spot in readiness if required".

(CC, 15th May 1858, p.5)

Whether it was the same Inspector Dade or not is uncertain, but there are stories that the first policeman sent to take up responsibilities in the area was murdered and his body disposed of in the kiln at the Burwell Chemical Manure Works. Clearly, some of the diggers had a deservedly fearful reputation. It has been said that the fair was often an occasion for a great fight between the locals and the "Irish", who, it has been suggested, made up some of the coprolite gangs. (Author's conversation with Major Jones, Far Gallions, Reach)

Such huge numbers migrating to the area included experienced Suffolk diggers. Villages like Bawdsey, Boyton, Newbourn and Sutton experienced population decline in 1861 owing to their coprolite diggers migrating to Cambridgeshire, *"where more available deposits have been discovered".* (CCRO 1861 Suffolk Census Vol.1.p.353) This was confirmed by the fenland historian, Mr. Wentworth-Day, who pointed out that the diggings

"...brought a good deal of prosperity to many Fen farmers and landowners and caused an influx of many hundreds of labourers from other counties, including Irish navvies, who were the cause of many bloody fights in the villages".
(Wentworth-Day, J. (1954), 'A History of the Fens,' Harrap)

The fact that the census did not record large numbers of Irish diggers suggests that if they were in the area, they had probably moved on to other work by April when the census was taken. Such a vast army of men would undoubtedly have had enormous social impact on the local communities, especially in terms of overcrowding. Most would have found lodgings in local cottages but others slept in farmers' barns, on the floor or table in the pubs or beerhouses, in tents by the roadside or in mobile barracks from the Crimean War.

A fascinating insight into the effect of the diggings on the area was recorded in an account of the life story of Annie Macpherson, who moved into Little Eversden in 1858 with her parents to stay with their aunt.

> *"Just at this time the discovery was made that the fossils embedded in the clay soil of that neighbourhood formed, when ground to powder, a valuable manure for the land. Within a week about 500 rough miners and labourers poured into the quiet little villages, and the pressing need was felt of efforts to civilise and evangelise these men, not only for their own sakes, but to save the rustics of the villages from the contamination brought about by the drunken and loose habits of these invaders of their peace, and the immorality induced by the absence of any provision for lodging and sleeping accommodation for this unprecedented addition to the countryside".*

(Birt, L "The Children's Home Finder', (1931), pp.9-14)

Many beerhouses were opened to cater for this influx of men and a wide variety of additional services introduced into the village's economy. (See author's account of Whaddon, Wimpole) Such was the demand for alcohol that the landlord of "The King William IV Alehouse" applied to the local Justices for a spirit license. This was refused because the Justices

> *"...were not prepared to have gin shops all over the place, with their accompanying female population, as had happened in Piccadilly, London".*

(Gathercole, op.cit.p.29)

In Horningsea the local public houses were closed early in an attempt to curtail problems. Whether the same practice was introduced here is unknown. (See author's account of Horningsea)

In nearby Bottisham, Rev. L. Jenyns, the religious academic and tutor of Charles Darwin at Cambridge University, read a paper on coprolites to a meeting of the Bath Field Club. He commented on how God had so blessed the fens as to provide such a profitable raw material, which improved people's lives but went on to say how they had brought immense wealth to his neighbourhood. He summed up the positive and negative impact of the diggings, commenting that they had

> "... led to a manifest improvement in their condition in some respects, while it has had an unfavourable influence upon it in others. The introduction of a new kind of labour, which may be carried on all through the winter, brings the men plenty of work, and from the nature of that work, higher wages than they were formerly used to. And this is greatly to the advantage of those men who are steady and provident. Earning from 15s. to 20s. a week, - even young boys of fourteen years getting 10s. for barrow work, - they not only live better, and are visibly better clothed on Sundays, but they are able to save. Further, some of the more intelligent labourers have become good mechanics, and have got to having the charge of steam-engines and other machinery; while the genius of the men generally has been much stimulated by endeavouring from time to time to discover the best and most advantageous methods of digging out the nodules, washing them, and carrying on other operations. The unfavourable result of these diggings is that drinking has increased. The men work very regularly their own time, and have their allotted beer - two or three pints a day - whilst engaged in it, which is

not much more than the labour requires. But leaving work every day at four in the afternoon, and on Saturdays always at twelve at noon, they have much time at their disposal, inducing idle habits, and tempting them to sit long at public houses on their way home.

...The diggings have also, to a certain degree, operated unfavourably for ordinary farm work. The labour is considerably affected in some places, though the scarcity of the men, at first much felt, has been partly corrected by immigration, families coming in from the woodland parts of the county to settle where the hands are most wanted. Formerly the price of labour was regulated by the price of wheat, now in the neighbourhood in which my informant lives, he tells me, for the last six or eight years, it has been affected simply by the supply and demand for labour, a principle before unknown in part of the country. All the able-bodied men go "a-fossilling" as it is called; and they scarcely ever go back to their former employments. The farmers, consequently, are obliged not only to pay a higher rate of wage than formerly, but to put up, in many instances, with the old and very young, the latter being taken away from school at proportionately early age, and thereby receiving detriment to their education. Boys of fourteen years get to consider themselves men in all their habits, and to assume an air of independence, not favourable either to their manners or morals, before they are much more than half grown up".

(Jenyns, Rev. L (1866) 'On the Phosphatic Nodules obtained in the Eastern Counties, and used in Agriculture.' Proceedings of Bath Natural History Field Club, pp.17, 112)

No evidence has emerged of Burwell diggers being charged with being drunk and disorderly but in February 1859 two of the men who worked at the coprolite mill in Burwell Fen appeared in court. They were accused of having attacked John Adams of Burwell between Rogers Road and Devil's Ditch. They had been drinking with him at the 'Rose and Crown' and followed him out. Adams fought them off but the case against them failed. There was not enough evidence to convict them. (CC. 12th Feb.1859)

Clement Francis' bill books show that in the first week of October 1859 Messrs. Ball had won agreements from Messrs Allix to work fields in Swaffham Bulbeck and Swaffham Prior. Edward Packard, one of Mr. Colchester's competitors in the manure trade, had also won an agreement from them to work their 9a.0r.34p. field in Burwell for £60 per acre. This was one of the earliest agreements where a royalty per acre was used. Land agents, aware of the difficulties involved in accurately weighing the thousands of tons leaving the coprolite works, encouraged landowners to change to a royalty per acre. This guaranteed a good income for the surveyors in Mr. Francis' business and elsewhere, as they could charge fees for having to measure the diggings twice a year, at Michaelmas and Lady Day.

The same year, when the seam was discovered under Burwell Charity land, the trustees allowed several local farmers to raise them. Mr Mason was given one licence and on March 23rd 1861 Messrs Ball got another. This latter agreement was unusual as it was on behalf of John Masters, a miller and merchant from King's Lynn. With the easy access via Burwell Lode it seems that the profitability of the enterprise must have attracted merchants from Lynn wanting to supply coprolites to manure manufacturers in other parts of the country. (CCRO. Francis Bill Books 1859 A-N pp.458, 474; 1860 A-N pp.21-2, 25, 121-2, 167, 469-70; 1862 A-N p.403)

The trustees didn't have the royalty per acre and instead

were paid between six and ten shillings (£0.30 - £0.50) per ton. What the Charity spent this revenue on is unknown but it would have been a great boost to their funds. The Ball's superphosphate was marketed widely. One of their advertisements in Kelly's Post Office directory for April 1860 stated that it had been, *"for two seasons fully and fairly tested in the counties of Norfolk, Suffolk and Cambridgeshire"*. (Kelly's Post Office Directory, Burwell, 1860)

Coprolites from Burwell Church Lands Charity

Jan 25 1859	98.5 tons at	10/- p.t.	£49. 5.0
June 7	118 ..	10/-	£59. 0.0
Sep 13	100 ..	10/-	£50. 0.0
Jan 3 1860	Coprolites		£40. 0.0
Jan 10 ..			£104. 2.6
Jan 10 Deposit Money, Coprolites			£40. 0.0
Mar 18 1861 Coprolites Messrs. Mason			£16. 3.0
Jun 14			£3.18.5
Mar 26 ..	Messrs. Ball		£60. 0.0
Mar 19	120.5 tons R. Ball	6/-	£36. 1.6
..	Messrs. Ball		£60. 0.0
	10.5 .. R. Ball	6/-	£3. 3.0
Total			£521.13.5

(CCRO. P18/25.103)

According to the 1861 census there had been a decline in Burwell and Reach's population over the decade. It had dropped by 100 to 1987. This may well have been due to men moving on to other parishes to work the diggings there. However, the industry here still involved considerable numbers. Richard Ball, 42, was described as a *"Coprolite and Manure merchant employing 108 men"* but there were only 32 men in the village actually described as being involved in the diggings. Maybe he included men he employed in Reach, Swaffham Bulbeck and Swaffham Prior. As only two men, one a labourer in the Manure Factory, the other an engineer in the Fossil mill, gave related

Lower Cretaceous Terrestrial Communities
a *Iguanadon* (Vertebrata: Reptilia: Archosaur – dinosaur)
b *Megalosaurus* (Vertebrata: Reptilia: Archosaur – dinosaur)
c *Hypsilophodon* (Vertebrata: Reptilia: Archosaur – dinosaur)
d *Acanthopholis* (Vertebrata: Reptilia: Archosaur – dinosaur)
e *Equisetites* (Pteridophyta: Calamites – horsetails)

(McKerrow, W.S.. (1978), *The Ecology of Fossils: An Illustrated Guide,*
Duckworth, p.297)

The Phosphate bed Community
(McKerrow, W.S.. (1978), *The Ecology of Fossils: An Illustrated Guide,*
Duckworth, p.286)

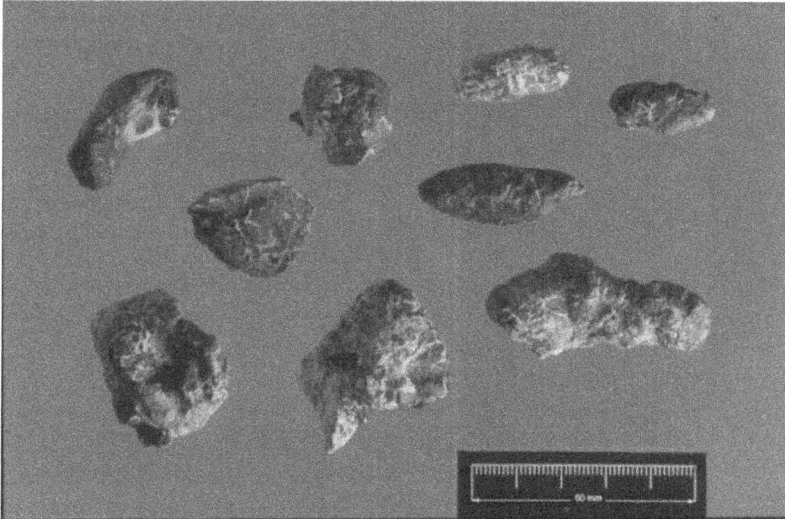

Cambridgeshire coprolites. (Photograph courtesy of Earth
Sciences Museum, Cambridge)

Cambridgeshire coprolites, thought to be 170 million
years old. (Courtesy of Tim Gane)

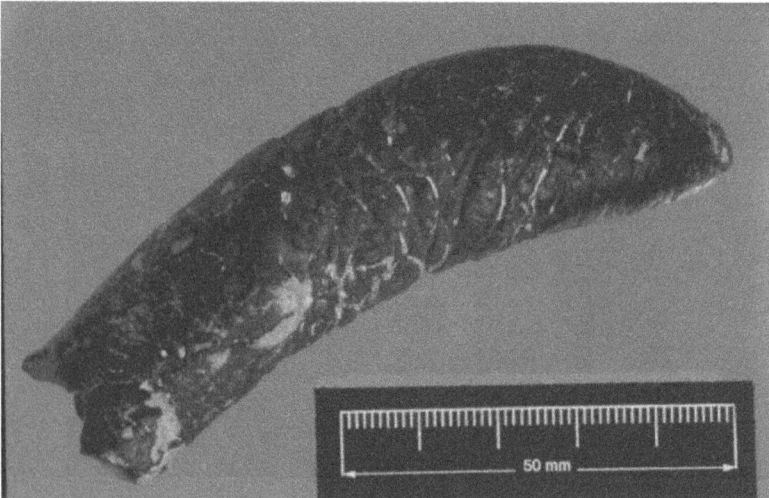

The Barrington coprolite
(Photograph courtesy of Earth Sciences Museum, Cambridge)

The Burwell Fossil Diggings — map of place locations

North →

Legend:
- • Coprolite workings
- o Location of Coprolite labourers
- ■ Manure Works

Place names shown on the map:

Soham, Wicken, Upware, BURWELL, Swaffham Prior, Swaffham Bulbeck, Reach, Bottisham, Stretham, Lode, Stow-cum-Quy, Fen Ditton, Cottenham, Waterbeach, Horningsea, Milton, Chesterton, Teversham, Cherry Hinton, Fulbourn, CAMBRIDGE, Grantchester, Trumpington, Westwick, Madingley, Coton, Barton, Haslingfield, Hauxton, Great Shelford, Little Shelford, Comberton, Harlton, Harston, Newton, Kingston, Great Eversden, Little Eversden, Orwell, Barrington, Shepreth, Meldreth, Thriplow, Fowlmere, DUXFORD, Wimpole, Croydon, Wendy, Knapwell, Melbourn, Wrestlingworth, Whaddon, Bassingbourn, ROYSTON, Abington Pigotts, Litlington, Ashwell Station, Gamlingay, Steeple Morden, Himsworth, Ashwell, Guilden Morden, Everton, Potton, Sutton, Edworth, Astwick, Storfold, Henlow, Arlesey, Shefford, Camyton, Meppershall, Upper Stondon, Lower Stondon, Clophill, Upper Gravenhurst, Shillington, Pirton, Millbrook, Ampthill, Ridgmont, Higham Gobion, Barton-Le-Clay, Eggington, Stanbridge, Billington, Slapton, Edlesborough, Leighton Buzzard, Brickhill, Dinton Bishopstone

Coprolite Diggings at Orwell, Cambridgeshire. 1860s – 1870s
(Courtesy of Cambridgeshire Collection W27.1J80 25358)

Coprolite Diggings in Cow Pasture, Abington Pigotts, Cambridgeshire, 1883
(Courtesy of Mr and Mrs Sclater, Abington Pigotts)

Photographs of the coprolite works on Sandy Heath, Bedfordshire, c.1882) The top photo shows women outside the sorting shed. The lower photographs shows a horse-powered cylindrical washmill. (Courtesy of Potton History Society)

Undated photograph of windmills in Bassingbourn, which, once the harvest had been milled, the millstones were replaced with buhr-stones to grind the coprolites. Horse-drawn carts brought the copro-lites along the road from diggings in nearby parishes.

Undated postcard of Bird's manure factory at Duxford, which was used to grind local coprolites and produce superphosphate.

Steam engine hauling coprolites from Whaddon to Shepreth Station c.1880
(Cambridge Collection Q AR J8 11029 Courtesy of Mrs Coningsby, Whaddon

Undated postcard of horse-drawn tumbrils carrying coprolites to the railway station at Millbrook, Bedfordshire.

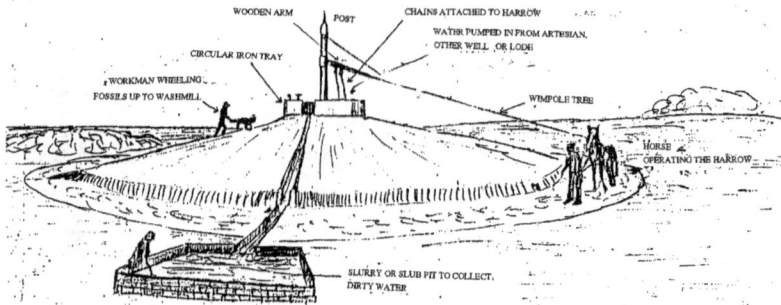

HORSE-POWERED COPROLITE WASHMILL

(Based on sketch in Richard Grove's Cambridgeshire Coprolite Mining Rush)

Undated photograph of a circular coprolite harrow
Cambridgeshire Collection: W27.1. KO. 19554).

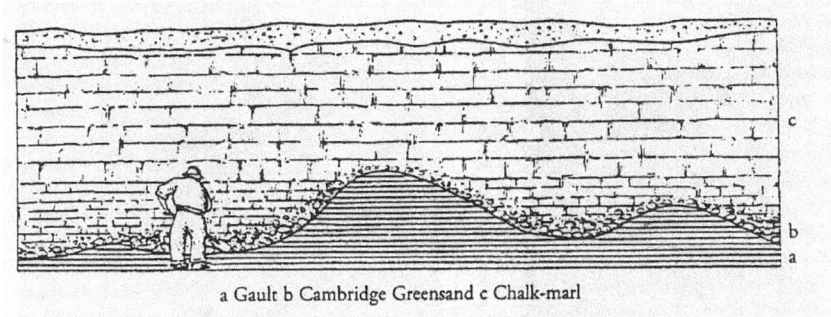

a Gault b Cambridge Greensand c Chalk-marl

View of a coprolite pit in Horningsea, Cambs.
(Jukes-Browne, A.J. & Hill, W. *Cretaceous Rocks of Britain,* Mem. Geol. Surv. 1903, p.194)

Undated photograph of coprolite diggers in Orwell, Cambridgeshire
(Courtesy of Sue Miller, Orwell History Society)

Photographs of the coprolite works on Sandy Heath, Bedfordshire, c.1882) The top photo shows women outside the sorting shed. The lower photographs shows a horse-powered cylindrical washmill. (Courtesy of Potton History Society)

Caricature of J.B. Lawes who patented the technique of dissolving coprolite and other phosphatic materials in sulphuric acid to produce superphosphate. He set up his own manure company, won contracts to raise coprolites and purchased others from diggings across
south-east England (*Vanity Fair* 8th July 1882)

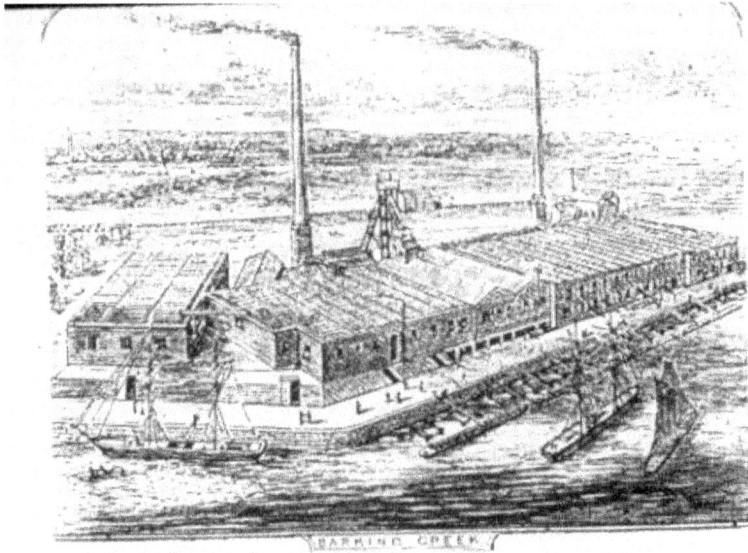

BARKING CREEK

LAWES' MANURE FACTORY, DEPTFORD CREEK.

(Courtesy of Lawes Agricultural Trust, Rothamsted Agricultural Station)

Undated photograph of coprolites being unloaded at Lawes'
Chemical Manure Works at Barking, London
(Courtesy of Rural History Centre, Reading University Neg. No.
35/23594)

R. & H. WALTON,

MANUFACTURERS OF ALL KINDS OF

MANURES,

EAST ROAD, AND COLDHAM ROAD,
CAMBRIDGE.

Blood Manure, Corn Manure, Turnip Manure, Mangold Manure,
SUPERPHOSPHATE OF LIME,
PREPARED NIGHT SOIL FOR CORN.

The following articles supplied in any quantity for mixing purposes:—

Half Inch Bones; Quarter Inch Bones; Sulphuric Acid;
Muriatic Acid; Sulphate of Ammonia; Agricultural Salt;
Soot; &c., &c.

Experienced Men sent out for mixing if required.
BONE AND MANURE WORKS,
EAST ROAD, AND COLDHAM ROAD, CAMBRIDGE.

Robert Walton's advert, Kelly's Post Office Directory 1864

Undated photograph of Edward Packard (1819 – 1899) who
founded Edward Packard and Company. In 1843 he began making superphosphate by dissolving old bones in sulphuric acid at Snape Mill. In
1851 he built Britain's first complete sulphuric acid and superphosphate
works at Bramford and went on to win coprolite agreements and purchase coprolites from across southeast England.
(http://www.yara.com/en/about/yara_centennial/heritage/
fisons_inter.html)

1861 photograph of William Colchester (1813–1898), one of the first manure manufacturers to use Suffolk coprolites. Had manure works in Ipswich, moved into Cambridgeshire fens in 1846, won coprolite contracts and purchased others from diggings across southeast England.
(Courtesy of Giles Colchester)

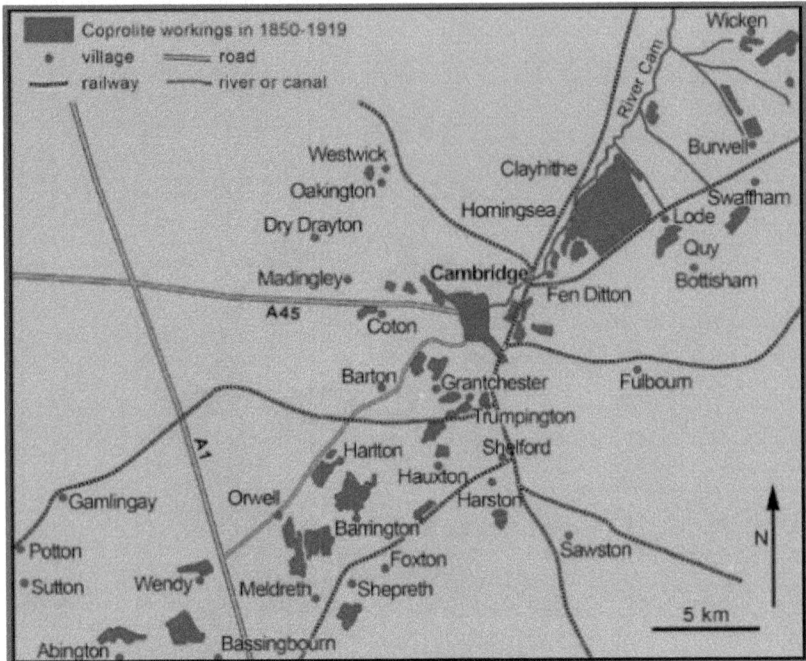

The extent of the coprolite diggings across Cambridgeshire
(Grove, R. (1976), The Cambridgeshire Coprolite Mining Rush,
Oleander Press)

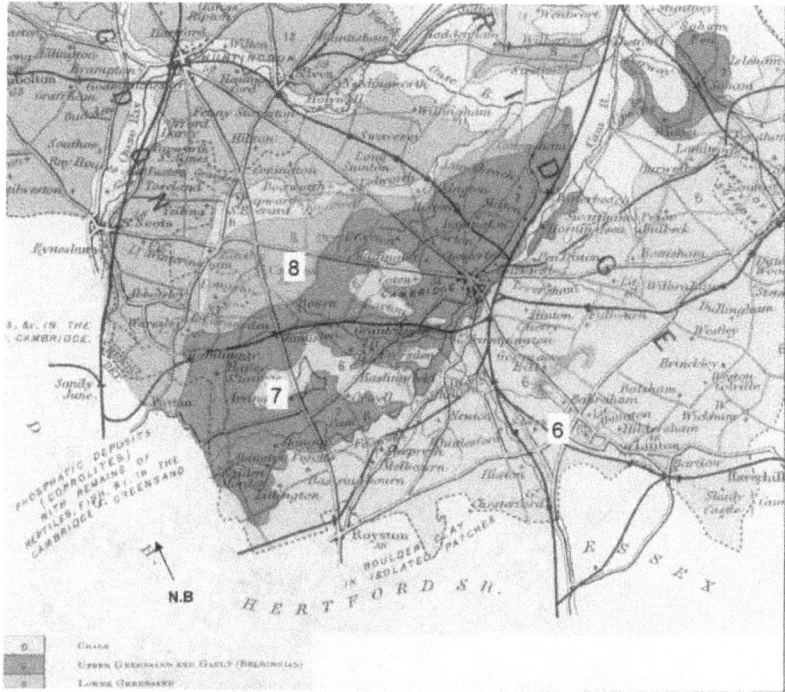

Extract from geological map of south-west Cambridgeshire after
Woodward (1904 based on Reynolds (Ian West 2001)
6 = Chalk; 7 = Upper Greensand; 8 = Lower Greensand

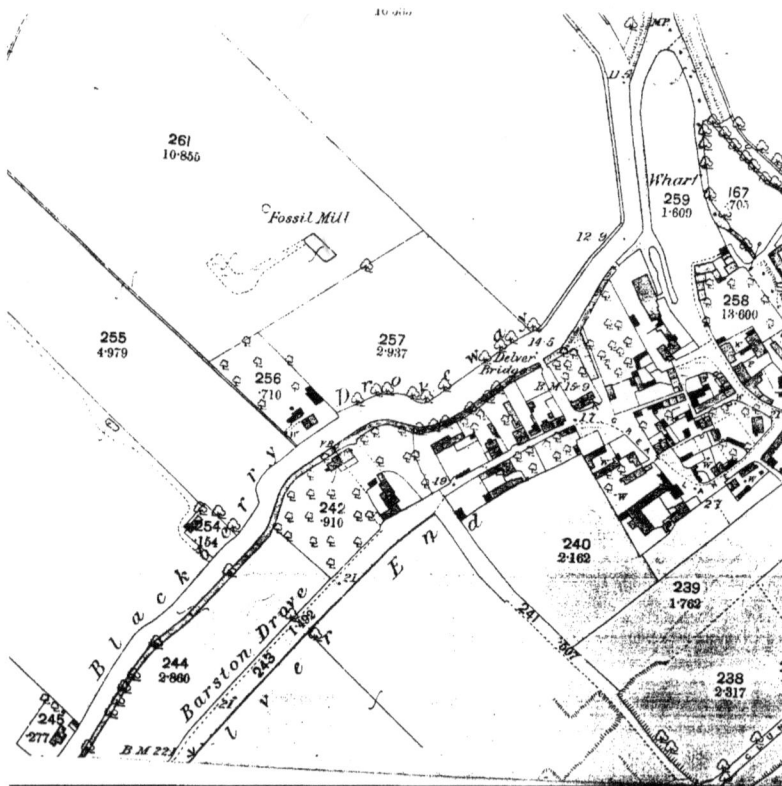

No map evidence of the diggings on Wicken Fen has come to light. This map shows one of the fossil mills near Reach. (1st edition 25-inch maps, Cambs.)

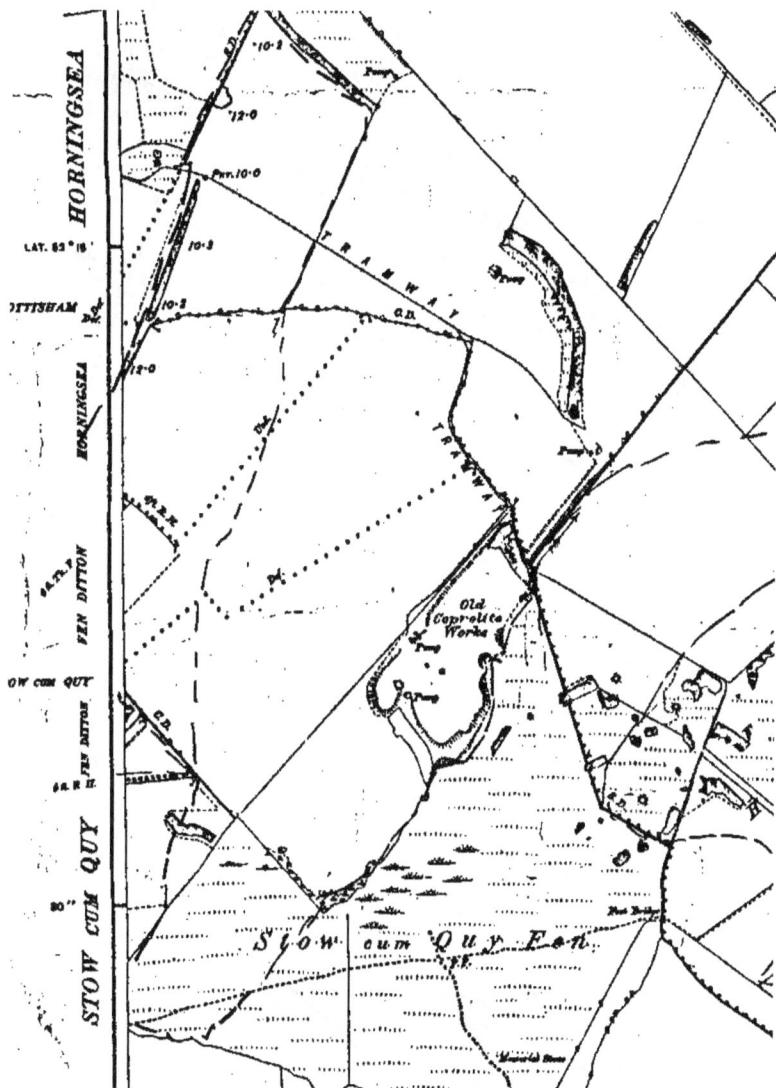

Extract from 1st Edition OS map showing Quy Fen coprolite works, water-filled trenches, old washmill sites and the tramway to the River Cam at Clayhythe

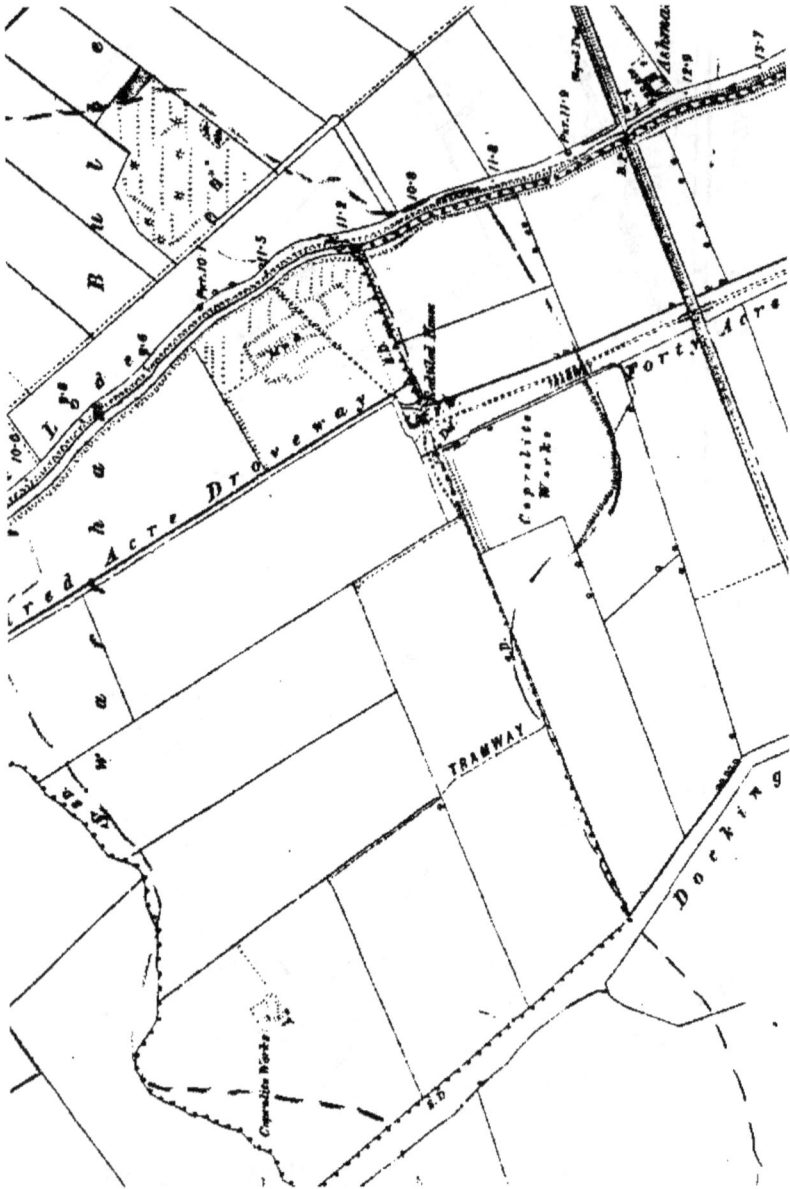

Two coprolite works and tramway marked on 1st edition 6-inch map of Cambs. at Redtiled House

Fluctuations in Coprolite Sale Prices

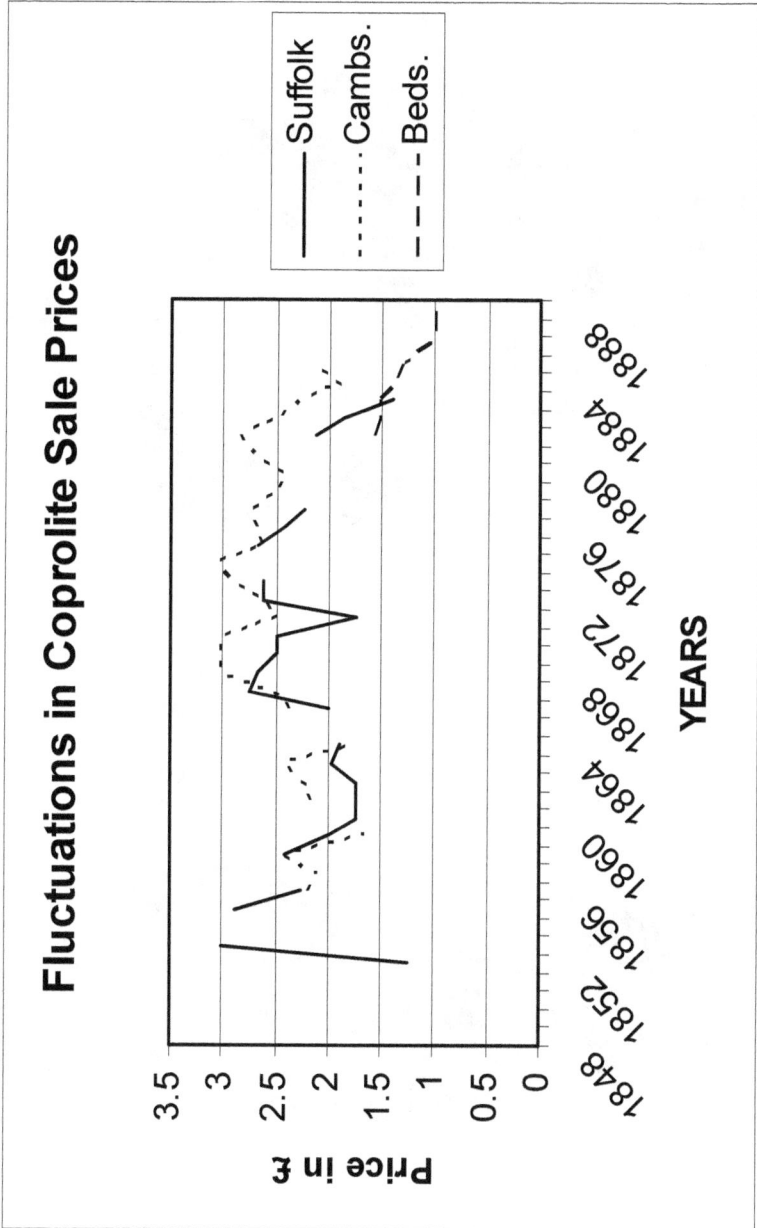

Undated photographs of William Colchester's Chemical Manure Works at Burwell.(Camb.Coll.W27.1,Y Bur.J9,23554; W27.1,Y Bur.J96 8402; W27.1,Y Bur.K32 4517)

Photograph of the Chemical Manure Works at Burwell in the 1880s after it had been purchased by the Prentice Brothers. (Cambridge Collection, Y.Bur.J9.23554.82/22/13)

Henry Fordham Esq
4 April 1873

①

IN FODDER FEN,

About ½-a-mile North of UPWARE, CAMBS.

A CATALOGUE OF THE

COPROLITE PLANT

INCLUDING—

1000 YARDS OF TRAMWAY

As laid, now in use at Mr. WILKERSON's Works, next
the River Cam,

TO BE SOLD BY AUCTION, BY

MESSRS.

NASH & SON

ON

FRIDAY, the 4th day of APRIL, 1873,

At 11 for 12 o'clock.

---

*May be viewed the day before and on the morning of Sale,
on application to Mr. Dennis's foreman.*

Catalogues may be had on the premises, at the Five-miles
from-anywhere public house, and of the Auctioneers, at
Royston.

ROYSTON PRESS—JOHN WARREN.

(CambRO. 296/B929.1; CUL.Royston Crow,4th April,1873)

POOR'S FEN, QUY,

CAMBS.

CATALOGUE OF ALL THE VALUABLE

COPROLITE PLANT

COMPRISING

About 20 tons of Tramway Rails, 40 Barrows, 10 Trucks, 70 Planks, 60 long Slurry Trough, 40 Hoisting Frames, 25 Crow-bars, 10 large Tubs, and Tanks, Washing Mill and Slurry Wheel, complete,

2 WELL-BUILT ENGINE HOUSES,

2 TIMBER-BUILT STABLES,

LARGE MESS ROOM,

AND

5 in. and 7 in. Centrifugal Pumps,

CAPITAL 10-H.P. PORTABLE ENGINE,

Quantity of Cast-iron Piping, 6 Driving Straps, and numerous other Effects.

WHICH MESSRS.

WRIGHT AND SCRUBY

Are instructed to sell by Auction, upon the Works, close to Quy Station, G.E.R.

ON TUESDAY, OCTOBER 30th, 1894,

At Eleven o'clock in the Morning.

Catalogues may be obtained of the Auctioneers, Cambridge and March.

J. Webb & Co., Printers, Alexandra Street, Cambridge.

(CCRO. Quy Fen Coprolite Works; Cambridge Weekly, 12th October,1894

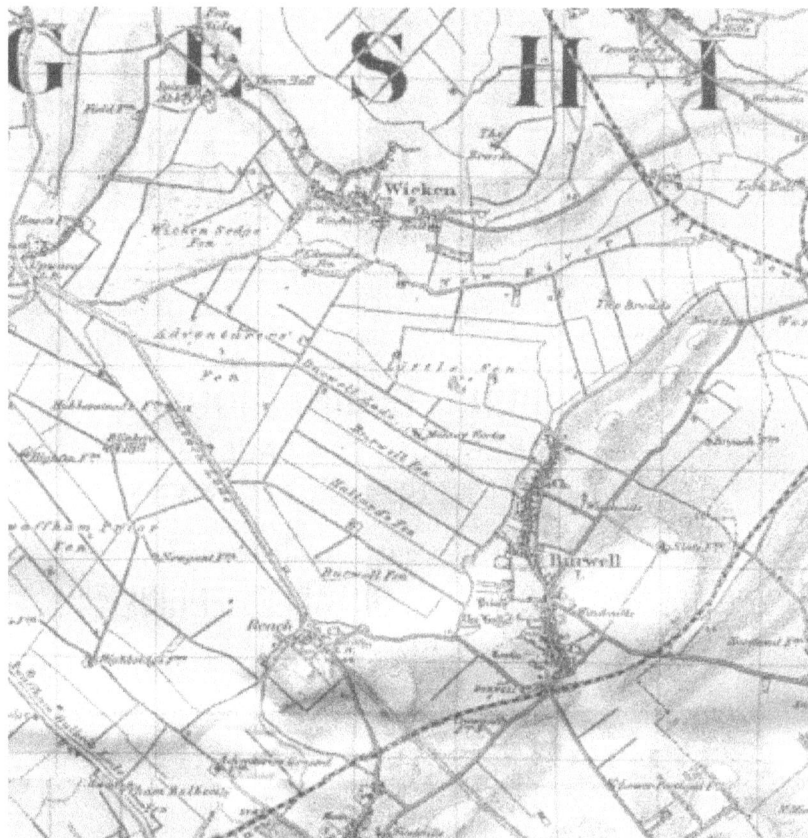

Extract of 1st edition 6-inch OS map of Burwell

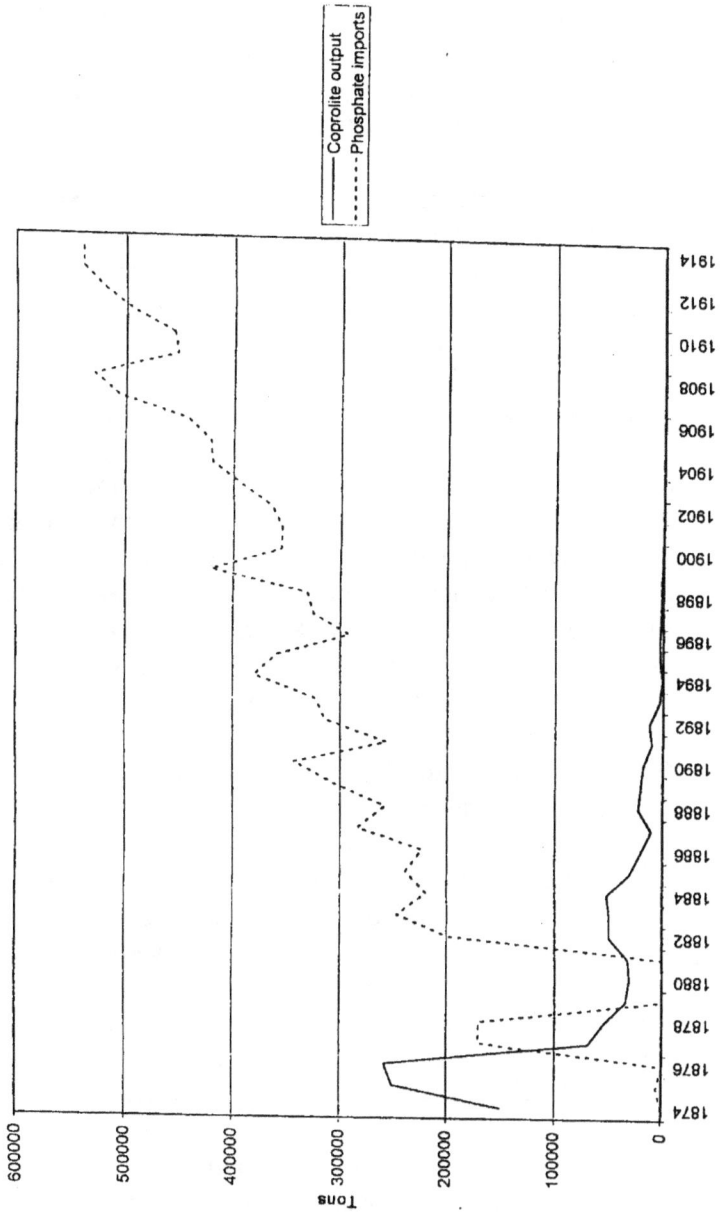

Coprolite Production and Phosphate Imports 1874-1914

occupations it seems likely that a lot of men and boys either described themselves as labourers or came from elsewhere. Their average age was 26.7, the oldest 52 and the youngest 12. It was very much a local occupation with 80.6% born locally and making up 8.6% of the total male population in Burwell of 368. (CCRO 1861 census, Burwell)

William Colchester at this time was living in Suffolk. He had used the wealth generated from the coprolites and manures to purchase Grundisburgh Hall. The local Suffolk trade directory listed him as not just a chemical manure manufacturer but also as a ship owner and boat builder. (Kelly's Post Office Directories, Ipswich) His social aspirations were high. Perhaps having ten children explains him having a governess, coachman, page, three housemaids, a cook and a kitchen maid. (Suffolk County Record Office (SCRO) 1861 census Grundisburgh) In line with many Victorian entrepreneurs who wanted to establish themselves in society, he invented tradition. He is reported to have filched the coat-of-arms of the Gloucester Colchesters to display on his tableware. A completely false family tree was written up purporting a descent from Oliver Cromwell, hence his second son being called Edward Cromwell Colchester. (Author's communication with Roy Colchester, Mendlesham)

When Colchester and Ball's Chemical Manure factory was first erected is unknown but the chimney shaft bore the date 1865. It must have dominated the view west of the town and been of significant importance to the local economy throughout the last century and well into the twentieth before it was eventually demolished in the late 1980s. (Conversation with owners of the works, Burwell)

In April 1861 a survey was made of 8a.0r.36p.of the Manor of Burwell Rectory land in Hallard's Fen, tenanted by John Kent. The Ely surveyor, Charles Bidwell was called in and he noted that

"...a portion of the land contains coprolites and 6 acres I have estimated can be worked and will yield about 120 tons per acre which at 4/- a ton royalty will produce £24 net profit. This amount I divide equally between the Lord and the tenant say of about £12 per acre".

(CCRO. Bidwell 18 p.89)

This was one of the lowest royalties recorded, unusual advice when up to a £100 an acre was being realised in some parishes. Was this a bit of dealing in favour of Mr. Kent? Hallard's Fen had a considerable number of the workings and it may well have been here where several serious accidents took place. The local correspondent for the Cambridge Independent Press reported

"**BURWELL ACCIDENT**. - On Tuesday last, a Wm. Beckworth, a labourer, was digging coprolites, he slipped and dislocated his leg; and as John Flack was digging coprolites, a large piece of earth fell on him, and he did himself serious injury".

(CIP, 22nd March, 1862,p.8)

Local doctors had a lot of work to do looking after injured diggers. It was said that not one escaped without a rupture or fracture and Addenbrookes Hospital in Cambridge had numerous broken limbs to deal with. (O'Connor, B. (1998), 'The Dinosaurs on Coldham's Common', Maythyme Press, Everton) During the January of the following year a discovery was made which may well have increased someone's income. Apart from a particularly good example of a fossil that could be sold to an avid geologist for a few shillings, there were the occasional archaeological finds. The Proceedings of the Cambridge Antiquarian Society included a paper by C. Babington on *"a Skull of Bos Primigenius"* which stated how

"Persons engaged in the digging for the so called "coprolites" near the village of Reche but in Burwell Fen found a head of that ox upon the chalk marl with a celt] embedded in its skull".

(Babington, C. (1863), 'On a Skull of Bos Primigenius associated with Flint Implements,' Proceedings of the Cambridgeshire Antiquarian Society (PCAS), Vol.2, pp.285-6)

A celt was a flint axe head, which shows evidence of Neolithic settlement in the area. In the same year a flint hammer was discovered in the mill used for cleaning the coprolites and was suspected of being used in prehistoric times for gutting fish. (Babington, C. (1863), 'On a flint hammer, found near Burwell,' PCAS. vol.2 p.201)

By the early-1860s the diggings had gradually extended across more and more of the skirt land with landowners quite happy to have their fields dug. On the 11th October 1863 the King's Lynn merchant, John Masters, won a further agreement from the vicar, William Cockshott and the Trustees of Burwell Church Land Charity. Again it was let through Thomas Ball. He was allowed to raise the fossils from 11 acres of Hallard's Fen, on the north side of the High Town Droveway, paying £405 for the privilege. (CCRO. P18/25.130; CCRO. Francis Bill Books A-N 1863 p.417)

It seems likely that it was from these workings that a Bronze Age hoard was unearthed by the diggers in 1867, about one mile Northeast of Reach. It consisted of eleven socketed axes, two chisels, three gouges, a hammer, five knives, two swords, a chape, seven socketed spearheads, six buttons, two bugle shaped objects and a number of rings and other items. (Journal of the British Archaeology Association, 36, 1880 pp.56-62) Where they are now is uncertain but it seems quite likely some artefacts remained in the diggers pockets and were never documented. The value of such treasures being found led Clement Francis to introduce a clause into the agreements that *"all Coins, Armour, Bones, Fossils,*

Relics, Antiquaries & Curiosities which shall be discovered shall be the property of the landowner". (CCRO. Bendyshe Papers T14/1; CCRO. Francis Bill Books 1868 A-N pp.391-2)

Richard Mason was willing to stake a lot on a new venture as in 1868 he was interested in coprolite land in Coton, fields just west of Cambridge. Demand for coprolite land had rocketed and surprisingly his offer of £130 per acre for the Charity Field was turned down. Thomas Thwaites Ball, who had taken over his father's business, also expanded his interests. In 1870, having finished the workings in Wicken, he ventured into the Stretham area where a new seam was being exploited. (See author's account of Coton, Wicken, Stretham)

On the 17th December 1870 "The Bushel" beershop at the Cross at the top of North Street, tenanted by George Davey, was put up for sale. Its access to the diggings accounted for the description that it was *"in a capital situation and doing a good trade".* Along with it were *"16 acres of productive land in Burwell Broads, close to a hard road and believed to contain Coprolites".* One lot, *"2a.3r.11p., known as the "Slipe" approached by the 2nd Drove",* was sold for £145 and the other, *"butting on the last, approached from the 1st Droveway",* was sold for £500 to a "J.P". Who J.P. was has not been determined but at that price it is almost certain the land would have been worked. (CCRO. 296B 919.41; Cambridge University Library (CUL), Royston Crow, Dec.1870, p.501)

A picture of how important the industry was in Burwell can be seen from an investigation of the 1871 census. There had been an increase of 119 since 1861 to 2106. This was a reversal of the trend but still a drop from the 2187 in 1851. Another farmer was recorded as involved, Robert Stephenson. As shall be seen in "The Times" article below, he was the tenant of the Crown lands. Aged 24 he lived at Causeway Pits Farm where many pits were noted on the first 25" OS map and presumably had both clunch and coprolites extracted. As well as being a landowner and farmer of 895 acres employing 24 men and 7 boys, he was also a

Maltster employing one man, and a coprolite digger employing 22 men and three boys.

Michael Mason, 26, of Burwell Hall, was the only Mason to describe himself as being involved. He was a farmer of 133 acres employing four men and one boy but also a coprolite digger employing 14 men and 17 boys. At the Parsonage, Salisbury Ball, aged 34, was a farmer of 365 acres employing 11 men, 10 boys and 3 women, a landowner of 144 acres, a Miller employing two men and a boy, and also a coprolite digger employing 36 men and 10 boys. The Ball brothers, Richard and Thomas of North Street, described themselves as coprolite, corn and manure merchants and another coprolite merchant living, at Lode Side, was Joseph Griffin, aged 27 from Reach. These, between them, employed 72 men and 20 boys, yet there were only 66 labourers in the census described as engaged in the fossil works, including two carters, two engine drivers and an engine driver at the coprolite works. Their average age was 25.7 with the eldest 50 and the youngest 9. 80% of them were locally born so from both censuses it can be seen that it was very much a young man's job, done mostly by local labour for local farmers.

Benjamin Stintom, aged 36, was the *"Chemical Manager"*. He lived at the Factory House, seen on the map in the illustrations. (O.S.Cambs.1st Edition 25" XXXV.11) He was in charge of eleven men described as *"labourers at the manure factory"*. Their average age was 24.2, the eldest 47 and the youngest 9. (CCRO 1871 census, Burwell) A photograph of the men at the works, reputed to have been taken in the early 1880s, shows a very mixed bunch of about forty men and boys. (Cambridge Collection, Y.Bur.J9.23554.82/22/13)

Little evidence has emerged of the diggings during the 1870s but they continued, as shall be seen later, on several farms. In 1873 a valuable deposit was discovered in the Lower Greensand at West Dereham to the north. It was on the estate of Hugh Aylmer, a large sheep breeder, who allowed two coprolite raisers, James Fison and Son of Thetford and Thomas Thwaites Ball and Co. to work it. (Kelly's Post Office Directories, Norfolk,

1879, 1883, 1892) Hardly a coincidence, in the same year the West Norfolk Manure Company was set up in Lynn. Their account books show they were buying in supplies from many fenland diggings. The Norfolk diggings further increased the coprolite traffic on the Ouse and Burwell Lode providing continued employment for many on the water and at Colchester and Ball's factory.

The early-1870s was a period of economic boom with investment in most sections of industry. The large demand for coprolite labour has been acknowledged as having an inflationary effect on the local agricultural economy. Apart from the decline in farm labour occasioned by the gradual introduction of farm machinery, many labourers were laid off during heavy rain or snow. With little or no job security, hired labourers in parishes along the coprolite belt who had been laid off after harvest would have been attracted by the higher wages offered by the coprolite contractors. Whilst some may have returned to farm work the stronger men would have been unwilling to return to lower paid farm work. In many cases farmers were compelled to raise the wages of the agricultural labourers to ensure their farm work was done. This reduced their profits and led to animosity between employers and labourers.

Incendiarism was a common occurrence in this area with crops, barns and even farmhouses set alight. Although the local press reported such cases there was no evidence that any coprolite diggers were involved. They had better job security as demand for coprolites was growing from the eighty manure companies that had been established by 1872. (See author's accounts of Ashwell, Potton, Madingley and Grantchester)

In nearby Exning, several years after wage improvements had been made in other parts of the country, there was discontent amongst agricultural labourers that they were still getting low pay. In early 1874 there were meetings to consider "combining", forming an Agricultural Union as was happening elsewhere in the country. A group of labourers went to the farmers demanding an extra shilling's pay (£0.05). The farmers refused which led to about 2,000 labourers in the area going on strike. The farmers responded by locking them out and refusing to employ any Union labourers at all. Those in tied cottages were threatened with eviction and many families' future was in jeopardy.

These were the days of "Captain Swing", the supposed leader of the agricultural labourers. Many attacks on farmers' property were attributed to him. The local MP, Mr. Ball, must have been involved, probably supporting the farming members of this agricultural constituency. Frederick Gifford, a reporter from "The Times" was sent to cover the incident and attended a public meeting held at Newmarket. An extract from one of his articles shed light on the conflicting views of farmers and labourers but also included details of what was going on in Burwell.

> "I do not think that a majority of farmers in the district would long resist the advance for which the men at Exning struck, and I am still more clearly of opinion, upon the lines they are now fighting, victory for the farmers will be more disastrous than defeat. The effect of the lockout, I believe, has been greatly to increase the strength of the Labourers' Union in the outlying villages. A mere attempt to gain a mere shilling a week on the one side and a refusal of it on the other, would have produced nothing like the sympathy and dogged feeling among the labouring class not hitherto connected with the Union by a refusal to employ all Unionists. Such a policy is bitterly resented as a denial of "the right of us poor men to stand shoulder to shoulder and pluck up a bit". "This was one man's way of putting it to me. "Our masters", said another, "will let us spend our two pence in getting drunk or in any other mischief, but we mustn't put it in the Union". Of course there is another point of view from which the lockout may be regarded as legitimate defensive warfare by the farmers. The men, however, cannot be made, or perhaps expected, to look

at it from any point of view but their own, and if the wholesale notices served on them to leave their cottages take effect, the exasperation and sense of wrong among them and their fellows for miles round will be such as one hardly likes to look forward to.

Some hundreds of labourers are employed in the Fens of Cambridgeshire in Coprolite digging, and this comparatively new industry competes with husbandry for labour. In Burwell, a parish adjoining the Exning, I visited some of these diggings today on land belonging to Mr Stephenson. The coprolites are a mass of petrified dung of extinct reptilia, found in the green sandstone formation, often mingled with bones and fossils. The surface soil where they are met with is black peat, which is about a foot deep. The coprolites lie here at a depth of six or eight feet, in layers about six inches thick, above the stiff blue clay, here called "gault". Fen land, the fee of which used to be worth less than 10/- an acre, now lets at the mere privilege of winning the coprolite at from 70l. to 200l. an acre. When it is dug into the peat topping is put carefully aside, and after the coprolites are extracted the ground is levelled and the peat mixed with the new surface soil. This made land - the local name for which is "slurry land" - is then worth 10/- more an acre as arable land than it was before. The coprolites are carefully washed to free them from the clay, and come out then like bits of blackish stone, generally rounded, from the size of a cherry stone to a pigeon's egg, sometimes bigger. They are valuable as manure, and in a factory close by, belonging to Mr. Ball, the son of the late member for Cambridgeshire, I saw the process of conversion. They are ground in mills to a very fine powder; but this is valueless for manure until it has been mixed with sulphuric acid, when the product becomes a soluble superphosphate, and is worth about 55s a ton. The coprolite diggers earn 17s or 18s a week, and at harvest time desert the diggings for the farm. They are in fact agricultural labourers; but the work is *much harder than that of the ordinary farm hand, though the hours are shorter and there is a Saturday half-holiday. The result, I am told, is that the number of recruits is small, and that the farm hands who have tried the work often go back to their old occupation at 13s a week. Another local industry is pursued by the Fen men, who dig peat for fuel or cut sedge for thatching, and are said to earn in this way an average of 20s. a week. The farmers say that the existence of these two industries in the district side by side with that of agriculture proves that the rate of wages paid to the farm hands must be a fair market rate, otherwise the farm hands would seek these two employments more readily than they do. The coprolite diggers are now turning Unionists. I may add that the Fen land in Burwell, where the coprolites are won, forms part of the Great Bedford Level. There is a navigable cut into the Cam, and the land is kept drained by pumping engines, the cost of which is defrayed by a drainage rate".*

(The Times, April 16th 1874)

This was the only reference to the Unionism of the diggers that has come to light. The local media, owned as it would have been at the time by the wealthier classes, would not have published stories encouraging strikes. A small independent newspaper in Bedfordshire reported a strike at coprolite works at Ashwell, Herts., which resulted in increased wages but there was no mention in the rest of the press. (Potton Journal, June 17th, 1871) Wages did increase during the early-1870s and with improved education and the availability of various publications there was an increased awareness amongst the working population about different wage levels in various parts of the country.

In the Bassingbourn area where one of Mr. Colchester's sons was working the local paper included the words of a song sung by the diggers. It gives a fascinating insight into the relationship between diggers and farmers.

COPROLITE DIGGING FOREVER
SUCCESS TO THE FOSSIL DIGGERS!

Come listen you farmers to what I do say,
We Coprolite diggers now can have fair play,
You once did us grind down, but now its our turn,
As we can get work and farm labour spurn!
We are jolly young fellows, that do not work fear,
We can work at the fossils, have a pot of good beer
With our spade and pickaxe we've no work to seek
We won't work for farmers for ten bob a week.

So good luck to all labourers wherever they may be,
The Coprolite diggers I mean for to say; .
Success to all men that can use the spade,
He's quite as well off as a man at his trade.

Remember old farmer you once had your way,
Of crushing poor labourers and make them obey,
But now we have plenty of work for to do,
So go to the d - - - l and all the fine crew;
Your sons & daughters with all their fine clothes
At the Coprolite diggers don't turn up your nose,
Remember t'was through us you have what you've got,
But still for all that you're a covetous lot.

But Willie and Johnny must follow their plough,
And Betty and Polly must go milk the cows; .
They must pull off their hoops and look to their dairy,
And not go a flirting with Tommy and Jerry; .
The farmer's sons too have got tears in their eyes,
For they'll have to work hard, and that is no lies,
Since Coprolite digging is now all the go,
They'll get no stone diggers to follow a plough.

There's many a man you'll say it's no lie,

That will make the poor farmers to sigh and to cry,
Thro' leaving their work when they're real good men,
But what is the use when you've nothing to spend; .
For the coprolite digging it now is alive,
They are sure to prosper which makes men to thrive,
You farmers are nothing but covetous elves,
You never spend anything, but want all for yourselves.

I've been to some works in famed Coldham's Lane,
And I've heard it repeated again and again,
That Poss will get married to red-headed Sall,
And I hope she will make him a very good pal; .
There's Tifey he loves a drop of good beer,
And Hello he is not behind, never fear,
There's Pegg too he's fond of a little wee drop,
And Blinkee he keeps the swankey beer shop.

There's no harm in what I'm going to say,
But if you should meet them by night or by day,
They will ask you a question and often repeat,
Hello! old fellow, how is your poor feet?
Where are you going on Sunday? they say,
Or anything else that comes in their way;
But still I respect them, they are hard working men,
And this is the reason I took up my pen.

So now I conclude with good luck to you all,
The lads and the men, the great and the small,
you are jolly good fellows wherever you be,
And where you got one bob, I hope you'll get three.

(Original in possession of the Sclaters, Abington Pigotts)

Mr. Gifford's article compared Burwell very favourably with the sheep farming area of Exning where labourers generally lived in little more than hovels. In Burwell two and three-bedroomed cottages with gardens were common. Demand for allotments was high with some farmers charging six pounds an acre for families to keep a pig and grow their own vegetables. This was 300% more than the highest agricultural rent!

There were some people in the area who suggested that outside agents had been sent from the Midlands to encourage the labourers to strike. One farmer from Kirtling reported receiving threatening mail.

> "Mr turner, you think you are going to friten us, you will friten yorself if you dont mind, and so will all farmers. Fairst week all we men are out of work we shall com upon you we be gen as we mean to go on. Your head will be taken off firs. We will make a smash the first week we are at ticket we cut off your head and set fire to your farms and we go rite thro the place, so you may look out for we mean to do it".
>
> (The Times, April 16th 1874)

Others felt that the labourers were otherwise a happy and contented lot. Augusta Stradbroke seemingly had not spoken to the same farm labourers as Gifford as she wrote,

> "The men are offered 17s. and 18s. a week all the year round, and have declined making more than that at the present rate of weekly wages and the extra pay given for hay and harvest. You make no mention, and probably have never taken into account, the low rent of their cottages. For good houses with three bedrooms, kitchen and parlour, and a quarter of an acre garden, they pay only 1s.9d. a week; for two bedrooms,, 1s.6d. a week. Also you say nothing of their many Benefit Clubs, clothing, coal and shoes &c., subscribed to unanimously and chiefly supported by their employers; their cottage garden shows and prizes; their dinners and treats at Christmas and harvest schools for their children, which until the passing of the late Act, were kept up entirely, and many are still, by their employers and landlords. All these are benefits and comforts which are not thought of, and would not be feasible in large manufacturing districts, but which add materially to the happiness and

unity of the two classes, - labourers and employers".

(Ibid.)

The tradition of harvest treats or "horkeys" had generally declined in many villages in favour of cash payments and those farmers that did continue the tradition tended to provide them for only the women and children. Benefit Clubs were thought of as a boon to the labouring classes but one labourer who was called out of the field by the farmer to answer Gifford's questions felt otherwise.

> *"How old are you, John?" "Sixty-one next birthday, Master". "How many children have you had?" "Twelve - nine living". You have always kept them without help from the parish?" "Yes -Thank God; I never had a penny from the parish in my life". The man, as I afterwards found out, had received a small money prize from the village Agricultural Society for bringing up a family without parochial relief, and he was now earning the usual 13s. a week". How long did you subscribe to that benefit club of yours, John?" - "Nigh upon five-and-thirty years". "It's gone now has it not?" - "Ah, Yes! That was a bitter bad job surely!" This poor man- happily still hale and strong - had paid into the club 1s.6d. a month out of his hard earnings - by what extraordinary thrift and self-denial one may easily imagine with his large family - and now all was lost. But for the sentiment of the thing he might as well have been idle and improvident; and if the children for whom he had worked so hard could not support him his only prospect in old age was the workhouse. The club had "broke-up", and he tried to tell us how and why. The story need not be repeated; but that, said my companion, "is the history of three-fourths of the benefit clubs about here".*

(Ibid.)

With the Times report on the lock out it would have been discussed by many across the country. The National Agricultural Labourers' Union held a meeting in Birmingham to discuss the event and its president, Joseph Arch, pointed out the justice of the labourers' case. A check for £100 to help the men and their families was donated by Birmingham Trade Council and Mr. Arch, *"prophesied that unless the farmers soon recognised the rights of the labourer and conceded him justice the land would soon be left with none to till it"*. The Union gave all the men 9s. a week from the subscriptions and actually encouraged those who wanted to emigrate, offering them free passage to Canada. (Ibid; Leighton Buzzard Observer 30th June 1874)

Whether the farmers did succeed in evicting the families and ban Union labour or whether the men succeeded in getting their increase was not revealed. As there was no compensation for loss of work or accidents whilst working, the men had to resort to helping each other. One report of coprolite diggers concern for their fellow workers was evidenced when this article appeared in the Cambridge Chronicle the following year.

> *"**BURWELL** - Collect for Addenbrookes. Coprolite men under S. Fison and T. Banyard have bestirred themselves and collected from the men employed in the separate works the sum of £5 7s.7d. Of this amount £2 19s. 7d Fison and 2 8s. Banyard. The men have requested that the money should be placed to the credit of Addenbrooke Hospital Fund as an expression of their gratitude for the care, kindness and attention shown to members of their works".*
>
> (CC.30th October 1875 p.8)

This suggests that Messrs. Fison and Banyard had leases in Burwell at this time but leases or correspondence has not documented it. They had extensive workings in nearby Horningsea during the 1870s, however.

In 1871 the Balls went into a formal partnership with William Colchester of Ipswich, whose coprolite interests spread in a wide belt across Suffolk, Cambridgeshire and Bedfordshire. They started advertising widely and the local trade directories at that time had them listed as coprolite merchants and artificial manure manufacturers. (Kelly's Post Office Directories, Burwell, 1875,1879; Grove, R. op.cit.p.9) In December 1875, confirming the extent of Ball's market, the invoices of the West Norfolk Farmers Manure Company in King's Lynn noted,

> "T.T. Ball, Burwell 30 tons of Coprolites at 55/- delivered to Manure Works in exchange for 50 tons Pyrites at 32/6 as per letter 13/12/1875 from T.T.B. £82.10s.0d".

(Norfolk County Record Office (NCRO) BR189.43 16/12/1875)

In spring 1876 they purchased 76 tons of Nitre Cake from Mr. Ball at 22/6 per ton, both shipments being made by lighters belonging to Mr. Dant. (Ibid. April 1876) With additional funds available from the merger it allowed considerable expansion of the factory on Burwell Lode where a fleet of steam barges was built up. These would have taken fertiliser, whole and ground coprolite down the Great Ouse to King's Lynn for transhipment, and to bring in coal, acid, other coprolites and imported phosphates for processing. All this must have dramatically stimulated the local economy, a trade described in D. Summers' book on the Great Ouse, as "a welcome addition to the dwindling volume of river traffic". (Summers, D. (1973), 'The Great Ouse', p.189; Grove, R.op.cit.p.37)

The photographs in the illustrations show the factory at various stages during its nineteenth century development. (Camb.Coll.W27.1,Y Bur.J9,23554; W27.1,Y Bur.J96 8402; W27.1,Y Bur.K32 4517) Having this factory, works in Ipswich and coprolite agreements in many counties Mr. Colchester became a major figure in the fertiliser business. In July 1872 he strengthened this position by joining one of a group of businessmen who paid £300,000 for Lawes Chemical Manure Company and its coprolite contracts. He was deputy chairman for eight years until 1880 when he took over as chairman. (Valence House Museum, Dagenham,Lawes Chemical Manure Co. Minute Books,1872-1880) £100,000 was used to set up Lawes Agricultural Trust at reportedly the world's first Agricultural Research Station on his estate in Rothamsted.

Few records of the industry have emerged for the 1870s but in a geological account of the area, Mr. Colchester gave the following estimate of coprolites he had raised since 1847. It was not clear whether these were his production figures from his Burwell works or whether they were from other parts of Cambs., Beds. and Suffolk. Regardless, one can see from them a clear picture of the industry's rapid growth during the 1850s, steadying out during the 1860s and 1870s and then falling dramatically in 1879.

Coprolite Production 1847 - 1889

1847 about	500 tons	1877 about	10,000 tons
1848	1,000	1878	10,000
1849	3,000	1879	4,000
1850	5,000	1880	5,000
1851	6,000	1881	5,500
1852	8,000	1882	5,500
1853	10,000	1883	5,500
1854	12,000	1884	7,800
1855	average	1885	6,000
1856	about	1886	4,000
1857	9,000	1887	2,000
1858	10,000	1888	3,000
1859	average	1889	5,000
	about		
	9,000		

(Reid, C. (1890), 'Nodule Beds,'Mem.Geol.Surv.p16)

Colchester's knowledge of the fertiliser business must

have made him aware of a growing trend during the mid-1870s of imports of cheaper, better quality rock phosphates, particularly from Charleston in the United States. (Suffolk County Record Office (SCRO) HC434/8728/402) By 1879 these imports exceeded local coprolite production and many coastal manure companies reduced or terminated their demand for local phosphates. This coincided with the beginnings of the agricultural depression at the end of the 1870s. Four consecutive years of wet weather and poor harvests caused financial problems for many farmers. These were intensified by the then Tory government's introduction of Free Trade that had allowed enormous imports of cheaper meat and cereals from the prairies of North America and the pampas of South America. Agricultural prices dropped. Farmers had little if any money, let alone interest in purchasing fertilisers. Mr. Colchester's London-based company prices for coprolites dropped from £3.60 a ton in 1878 to £2.45 a ton in 1879. Their purchases stopped entirely in 1880. (Valence House Museum, Dagenham, Lawes Chemical Manure Co. Minute Books,1878-9)

Although his production figures show a 60% drop in 1879, there were still 4,000 tons produced. Were these from the Burwell Chemical works? The freight costs of bringing in the American phosphate by rail or barge to the inland factories may help explain the continued, albeit lowered, demand.

Although none of the Burwell Chemical factory's records have come to light it is quite likely bargees, labourers, carters etc. would have been laid off and fertiliser production reduced. Evidence shows that prices for Cambridgeshire coprolite dropped from an average £2.73 in 1878 to £2.48 in 1879. The fact that some directors and shareholders had strong interest in coprolites may well explain the continued demand. One of William Colchester's sons, also called William, was in charge of an extensive operation in Abington Piggots and Bassingbourn where he had a coprolite factory. It made much of the plant and machinery required in the industry. The chairman of the Farmers Manure Company of Royston had coprolite works on his farm in Bassingbourn. (O'Connor, B. (1998) 'The Dinosaurs on

Bassingbourn Fen', Maythyme Publishing, Everton)

In many areas workings were abandoned or the work reduced. What happened on Messrs. Fison's and Banyard's works is not known. Where the work stopped, pits were left unlevelled and allowed to fill up with water. Machinery was left locked up in sheds or sold. A vital source of income for the town and the surrounding area was lost.

The effects of the depression were widespread. Rents went unpaid, many tenant farmers fell into arrears and were thrown off the land. Some labourers and their families emigrated. Others left the area to find work in the large towns. There was severe distress in the area felt by most sections of society. Mr. Bidwell's survey of an estate in Burwell and Wicken in 1879 confirmed the problem. He stated that,

> "Turf used to be raised at £20 per acre and the clay was of excellent quality & makes capital material but the work has been discontinued, I take it because of the difficulty of commanding labour".

(CCRO. Bidwell 33, March 1879)

Things had not improved by 1881 when the vicar, William Cockshutt, in a note to the bishop, pointed out that, "The value of the Glebe diminished from £360 because of the present agricultural distress. This year the net income is £320". (CUL. Ely Diocesan Register C3/28)

However, by April 1881 there was an upturn in the industry. Only sixteen months after Mr. Colchester took over the chair of Lawes Chemical Manure Company, he informed the directors that because Messrs Wyllie, Teacher and Gordon, one of the shipping companies bringing in American supplies, were

> "very much behind in their deliveries of Phosphates under contract he had been compelled to purchase 2,800 tons of

coprolites at considerably increased prices and also to purchase 250 tons of superphosphate to enable him to fulfil contracts made last autumn".

(Lawes Chemical Manure Co. Minute Books, II, 1880, pp.258-9)

This renewed demand for the coprolite, probably from his own and his family's workings, would have maintained the workforce in what was otherwise difficult economic circumstances. This gradual revival was evidenced from Mr. Colchester's figures showing his purchases increasing almost 30% from 4,000 in 1879 to 5,500 in 1881.

The 1881 census showed that, over the decade, Burwell's population had fallen by 57 to 1,949. The coprolite industry had lost its place as a major local industry as there were more turf cutters than fossil diggers! Robert Stephenson was not described as involved. He had invested his coprolite profits as he farmed an extra 500 acres employing larger numbers of men, women and boys. Salisbury Ball farmed a smaller acreage but was still engaged in milling. He described himself as a *"Coprolite raiser employing six men and two boys"*. George Peachey described himself as farmer and fossil digger, suggesting he may well have been raising them from his own fields and selling them to the chemical works.

Only five local men described themselves as fossil diggers. Their average age was 29.2, slightly older than in 1871. The eldest was 45 and the youngest were two 18-year olds. All but Edward Peachey from Swaffham were born in the parish and he was a boarder with George. Thomas Ball was described as chemical manufacturer, employing 33 men but only 16 men and boys in the parish described themselves as involved. Maybe the others came from other parishes. There was a coprolite grinder, coprolite miller and engine driver at chemical works and the average age of those at the works was 36.7 with the eldest 52 and the youngest 12. (CCRO. 1881 census, Burwell) The photograph in the illustrations, reportedly taken during the 1880s, may well include some of these characters.

Although Mr. Colchester's figures show a steady increase during the early 1880s to 7,800 tons in 1884, demand for coprolites plummeted to 2,000 tons by 1887. The reduction can be explained by several factors. By this time the most accessible seams had been exhausted. The deeper pits incurred higher labour and pumping costs. The coming of the railway in 1884 would have facilitated easier access of the imported phosphates. Taking 250 tons as the average yield per acre one can then see that only eight acres were worked in 1887 compared to forty eight a year when the industry was at its height in 1854. Linked to this decline Messrs. Colchester and Ball branched into the brick industry in the 1880s with clay pits being dug to the north of the factory and a tramway linking them to a line which ran by the Lode. Henry Empson Cox was taken on as the managing clerk and many of the skilled fossil diggers would likely have been employed in these new works. With the growing populations of the large towns and the modernisation of local housing there was a great demand for white facing bricks in the construction industry. The tunnel from Ely to Warren Hill was lined with bricks from the works. (Kelly's Post Office Directories,1888,1892; SCRO   HC434/ 8728/152)

In the early 1880s Mr. Colchester disposed of part of his manure interests to Prentice Brothers of Stowmarket. He kept his interest in the Burwell works and in 1886 his son, George, joined Mr Ball. Under the name, Colchester and Ball, the company developed rapidly. Figures show that their purchase of coprolites stopped in 1887 showing their reliance for the new phosphates from overseas. Instead they invested in the cement industry. Many coprolite contractors ventured into this new industry in the 1880s exploiting the local chalk marl.

Burwell, Cambridge 23 July 1888
Dear Charles Edward,

By the bye Jane Cobbold lives in the next parish.
Charles Bye made her an offer of which she did not
forget to remind us the other day & added he wrote
to congratulate her on their marriage which she
thought no good of him. Ned's wife is bringing Ned
his fossil in deposit of natural clay fit to make
Portland cement & is going strong....
I have got out of all business except my
directorships which luckily gives me a thousand a
year - the
precious boys have taken possession of the
businesses and I am glad to see them thriving."
Yours very truly

W Colchester
(Correspondence in possession of Giles Colchester,
London)

Whilst there are no records of coprolite diggings in Burwell during the 1890s there was another slight revival in Quy Fen when Sarah Francis, Clement Francis' widow and Lady of Quy and Fen Ditton Manor allowed a committee of 60 unemployed men to raise them without paying any royalties. This philanthropy during difficult times led other landowners to open new workings at Horningsea, Stretham and Soham. It is quite possible they were processed in Burwell but unfortunately there are no records to confirm it. (See author's accounts of Soham, Quy, Horningsea, and Fen Ditton)

The 1891 census showed a reversal of the population decline seen in 1881. The population had increased by 49 to 1998. George H. Colchester, now 33, had taken over as *"Chemical Manure Manufacturer"*. He was well enough off to live on North Street with three servants. There were twenty-two men engaged as labourers in the factory with jobs including engine driver, coprolite grinder, timekeeper, plumber and fireman. They even had a "Manure School". Their average age had risen to 37.8, older men pleased to have at least a steady income when many of the younger men had left. (CCRO. Burwell 1891 census)

William Colchester resided at Burwell House, which was probably improved using the profits of his business. Following his death in 1898, his sons, William, Edward and George, continued the tradition of supplying local farmers with fertilisers into the 20th century.

During the First World War manure companies experienced difficulties in securing overseas phosphate supplies. German U-boats and warships threatened a naval blockade, which prompted the Ministry of Munitions to investigate the possibility of reopening coprolite workings. A major operation got underway in Grantchester and Trumpington. It was reported that 3,000 tons were raised in Horningsea during the war but this hasn't been confirmed by other sources. Whether they came into Burwell is not known. (Cambridge Village Book, Women's Institute)

Immediately after the war the Colchesters sold off both the manure and brick business to Prentice Brothers. (Grove, R. op.cit; 'The Early Fertiliser Years,' Fisons's Journal No.77 December 1963. The Suffolk fertiliser business of Fisons subsequently took over Prentices but the connection between the Suffolk Fisons and the Fisons in this area has yet to be confirmed.) Conditions in the factory were said to have improved dramatically. Records of some of those employed have survived and help shed light on the working conditions of the men. The Prentices introduced a week's paid holiday per year and a day rate for a 48-hour week of £1.87. The superintendent, Mr Gathercole, was a keen local historian and he wrote a brief history of the company in 1959. (Gathercole, op.cit.) His interviews with some of those employed in the nineteenth century have helped shed light on the working conditions of the men and boys. It was clear there was antagonism between them and their employers. The Colchester family, it was said, were *"hard drivers of men who watched every penny and used anything that could bring in a penny"*. (SCRO. HC434/8728/152) One labourer was so exhausted that he regretted ever having had to come to work. *"Slave drivers and hard with the cash"*, he said of them. *"Cruel work that were"*, said another, describing the crushing of pyrites. He had been unable to wheel the 4 cwt. barrow-loads from the barges to the bank. The men were allowed four pints for clearing the bottom of a barge, which suggests that there was alcohol available on site. Rates were 4d. (£0.02) for every ton moved with sixpence (£0.025) for the final ton. It was particularly dusty work which led to many complaints from the men but Colchester was reported as saying *"Let them be blinded, we can soon get another lot"*. (Ibid.)

At Christmas time the men were given pork or beef as a present, depending on which was the cheaper, four pounds for the married men and two pounds if they were single. From all accounts the company also acted as a local knacker. Dead animals, they said, were boiled in an old pot, the fat sent away and the bones and other residue added to the "den". Often a piece of meat was put in the pot and boiled with vegetables as their stew for a whole week. (Ibid.)

There was little care in those days for safety regulations. Men were often hurt and work in the "den" or acid chamber was described as a terrible job. As well as the normal additions of fossils, bones, phosphates and acid, old leather and the contents of the four lavatories were added. For this work the men were paid a guinea (£1.05) a week. The men reported using what they termed "blue fossils" during the First World War after they had been washed in the yard. As there were reports of diggings starting again in the fens during this period there is the possibility the coprolites were brought in by barge and processed here. (Ibid. See author's account of Horningsea.) It was said that the original supply of rock phosphate came from the Somme Valley in France and there is evidence of what were called French coprolites being imported as early as 1880. (Valence House Museum, Dagenham, Lawes

Chemical Manure Co., Minute Book 1880)

During the Second World War American "Triple" phosphate was used which proved the worst unloading job of them all as it caused profuse bleeding of the nose. (Suff.RO.HC434/8728/152)

An additional part of the company's business portfolio was barge building. At one time they owned thirty barges and four tugs and employed five boatwrights, two carpenters and a wheelwright for carts. During the off-season the barge bottoms were tarred and in January they were loaded up with fertiliser for delivery to the Fens. At Denver Sluice horses took over from the tugs as their wash caused bank erosion in the fen country. Although it seemed there was some environmental awareness in those days there must have been considerable effluent dumped into the Lode from the factory and gases escaping into the atmosphere. The addition of superphosphates to the soil over the past century has left its own disturbing legacy.

There were reports of silt from the dredging of King's Lynn harbour being brought down to be used on the fields and later road stone for the local council. Carrying sugar beet for the sugar industry also provided a useful source of income and, by the time the barging side of the business was eventually sold, they were carrying 3,000 tons a year. Materials were unloaded by the men up deal planks with two men at the top to pull the carrier up the last few feet. Three horses were used to pull the loaded carts into the works which could not take more than five bags (10 cwts.)

As it was just a dirt track from the works to the retail yard in the village, just opposite Burwell House, goods were brought in by barge. The carts used to go off into the fens and the woodland country. Work started at four or five in the morning and the drivers were often not back before 9 or 10 at night. As the roads were all unlit until gaslights arrived the horses picked their way, knowing when to stop at the right farm or public house. There were many reports of drivers being fined for being asleep and not in full control of the horses. Mr. Sangster was caught speeding in Newmarket and boasted his horses could do ten miles in two hours. (Ibid.)

Despite the few records that have come to light of this addition to Burwell's economy the diggings and the chemical manure work must have played a significant part in providing a good income for many labouring families, as well as those of the contractors, farmers and landowners. Little now remains to remind one of the coprolite industry but this short account should help keep alive the memories of those whose working lives were dominated by this unusual activity.

www.ingramcontent.com/pod-product-compliance
Lightning Source LLC
Chambersburg PA
CBHW071456070426
42452CB00040B/1536